150 Best Eco House Ideas

150 Best Eco House Ideas

COLLINS DESIGN
An Imprint of HarperCollinsPublishers

HarperCollins books may be purchased for educational, business, or sales promotional use.
For information, please write: Special Markets Department, HarperCollins*Publishers*,
10 East 53rd Street, New York, NY 10022.

First published in 2010 by:
Collins Design
An Imprint of HarperCollins*Publishers*
10 East 53rd Street
New York, NY 10022
Tel.: (212) 207-7000
Fax: (212) 207-7654
collinsdesign@harpercollins.com
www.harpercollins.com

Distributed throughout the world by:
HarperCollins*Publishers*
10 East 53rdStreet
New York, NY 10022
Fax: (212) 207-7654

Editorial coordinator: Simone K. Schleifer
Assistant to editorial coordination: Aitana Lleonart
Editor and text: Marta Serrats
Art director: Mireia Casanovas Soley
Design and layout coordination: Claudia Martínez Alonso
Layout: María Eugenia Castell, Guillermo Pfaff Puigmartí
Cover layout: María Eugenia Castell

13 14 15 SCP 10 9 8 7 6

Library of Congress Control Number: 2010928178

ISBN: 978-0-06-196879-2

Printed in China

© R&Sie(n)

CONTENTS

Introduction

An increasing scarcity of resources; global warming, partly caused by emissions from the construction industry; and the rising price of raw materials are leading architects to consider a series of good building practices to achieve a sustainable environment.

The road to responsible architecture depends on the efficiency of buildings and their carbon footprints. There are two main building systems in ecological architecture; they are known as passive and active systems. The former refers to strategies that make maximum use of the conditions of a location (its climate and orientation), insulation, and the thermal inertia of materials to make heating and cooling buildings as natural as possible. The latter turns to technology for optimal thermal comfort. Currently, the best-known active energy-supply systems are: photovoltaic and thermal solar, geothermal, and wind energy, although there are others, such as hydraulic and tidal power.

Another major sector in the field of sustainable architecture is prefabricated homes. Formerly associated with a uniform aesthetic, they have improved their individual design features in recent years. Among their benefits over traditionally-built homes are: a greater control of building processes and the lowering of costs and the environmental impacts of construction.

Today, reducing the ecological impact of construction is primarily in the hands of those directly involved (architects, designers, and homeowners), as well as government officials who deal with legislation concerning environmental preservation measures. A home designed logically for healthy living and energy self-sufficiency not only achieves the best habitat conditions for its occupants, but the construction of such homes can be a critical tool for halting the environmental crisis.

Passive Energy Strategies

Twin House

Architect: UdA
Location: Revigliasco, Italy
Year of construction: 2008
Photography: Carola Ripamonti

This two-story house faces south and uses a ventilated facade method. Its structure is composed of brick and glass surfaces incorporating a patterned adhesive film. The external surface is clad with thermoset phenolic resin wood panels and a synthetic grass layer covering the exposed parts.

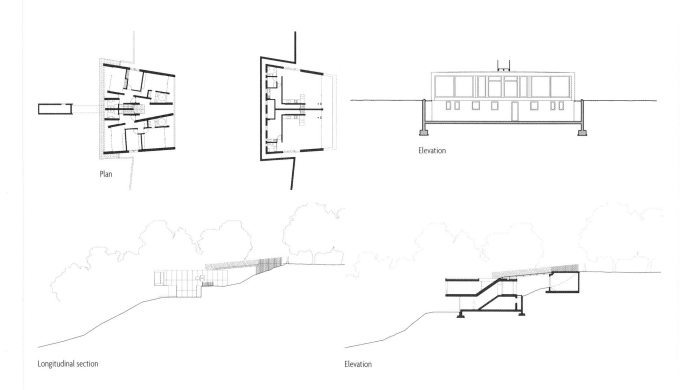

Plan

Elevation

Longitudinal section

Elevation

001

A building's orientation should be influenced by its source of energy. Glazed openings and long facades should face south.

A walkway was built to give access to the interior of the house from its roof.

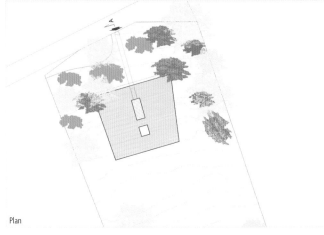

Plan

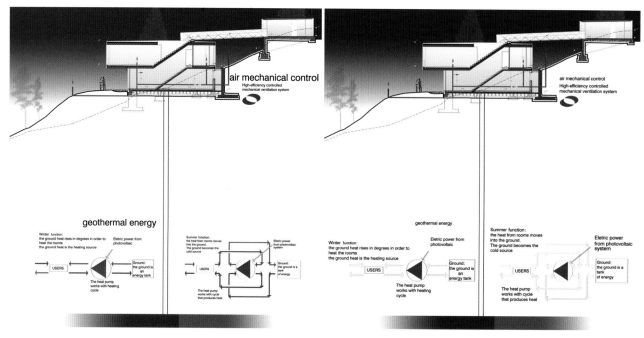

Energy diagrams

002

Geothermal heating and cooling extracts heat or sends it into the ground by means of collectors buried in the subsoil.

Farmhouse

Architect: Einar Jarmund, Håkon Vigsnæs, Alessandra Kosberg / Jarmund/Vigsnæs AS Arkitekter MNAL

Location: Toten, Norway

Year of construction: 2008

Photography: Nils Petter Dale

This house was built next to a vacant farm. The planks, part of the structure of the old farm, were reused for the new house. The main section faces south to allow light to enter in winter. A small roof garden regulates the temperature inside, acting as a heat source in winter and a temperate zone in summer.

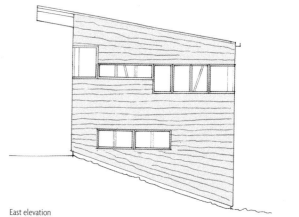

East elevation

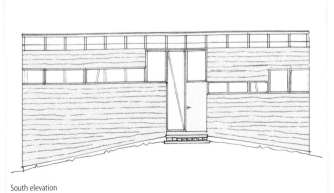

South elevation

003

Glazed openings in walls are thermally weak. Low-E insulating glass helps compensate for this.

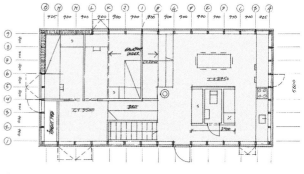

004

Natural energies used in bioclimatic designs are cyclic. They produce high peaks at certain times and are totally absent at others.

Plan

Chen House

Architect: Casagrande Laboratory
Location: Sanjhih, Taipei County, Taiwan
Year of construction: 2008
Photography: Casagrande Laboratory

Chen House was built on land with harsh environmental conditions: extreme heat, high winds, periodic floods, and seismic activity. Its bioclimatic strategies are based on ensuring the flow of air from the river during hot days. The house is elevated above the ground to avoid flooding.

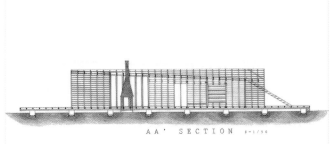

Longitudinal section

The facade has been strategically designed to capture breezes. A fireplace is used in the winter for heating and cooking.

BB' SECTION s=1/50

Transversal section

005

The use of locally sourced materials is economical because fuel and CO_2 emissions from transportation are not added to their cost.

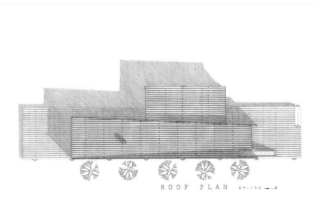

R O O F   P L A N   s=1/50

Roof plan

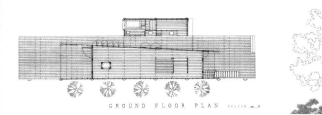

GROUND FLOOR PLAN

Ground floor plan

006

More than 50 percent of energy exchanges between a building and its environment are produced by air renewal.

Casa Mar Azul

Architect: María Victoria
Besonías, Guillermo de Almeida,
Luciano Kruk/BAK Arquitectos
Location: Mar Azul, Argentina
Year of construction: 2004
Photography: Gustavo Sosa
Pinilla/Summa+

This house, situated in an area with a humid microclimate, was created as a concrete prism, achieving a low cost of implementation and maintenance. Located in an area with more than forty pine trees, it stands on a pine-treated platform to avoid destroying the ecosystem. It has a water tank to collect rainwater.

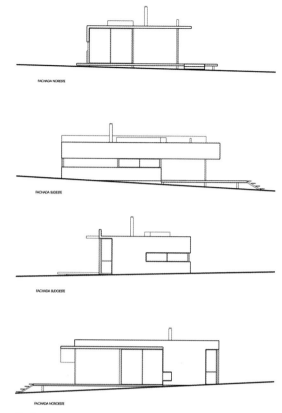

Elevations

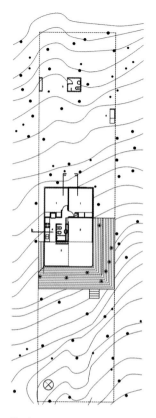

Site plan

007

Good building practices prevent unsightly alterations to a building's surrounding environment and preserve its biodiversity and natural resources.

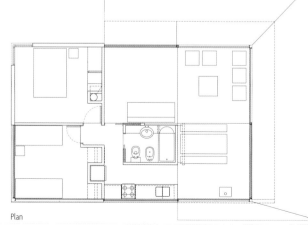

Plan

008

The use of highly-thermal materials, such as concrete, in bioclimatic systems maximizes energy storage.

Furnishings were made from Canadian pinewood recycled from engine packing crates.

R&Sie(n) has just completed the design of a private laboratory, which was built with twelve hundred hydroponic ferns and three hundred glass blown pods. Assembled on a flexible structure away from the facade, the fern/pod system is designed so that each of these plants collects rainwater through a drip system. The glass blown pods also reflect natural light into the interior spaces of the building.

Architect: R&Sie(n)
Location: Paris, France
Year of construction: 2008
Photography: R&Sie(n)

	longueur	quantité
Façade	30*30mm	486
Pignon nord	30*30mm	154
Pignon sud	30*30mm	41
Toiture	30*30mm	308
	Total	989

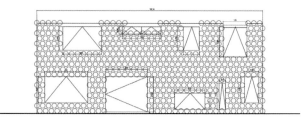

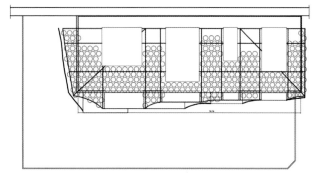

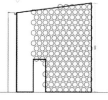

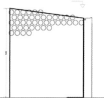

Vegetation scheme

009

Hydroponics is a method of growing plants using mineral solutions. It does not require soil.

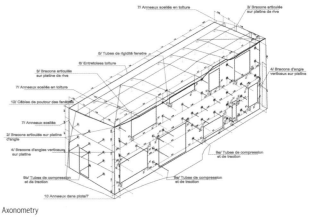

Axonometry

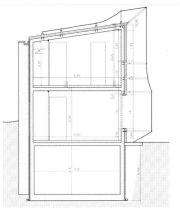

Cross section

010

Green facades are low
maintenance because weeds
are unable to invade the vertical
surface. Annual pruning,
however, is required.

When sunlight comes into contact with
the three hundred bulbous glass features,
it is projected into the building's interior.

House 205

Architects: David Lorente,
Josep Ricart, Xavier Ros,
Roger Tudó/H Arquitectes
Location: Vacarisses, Spain
Year of construction: 2008
Photography: Starp Estudi

For minimal impact on its surroundings, House 205 sits on an existing rock platform. A prefabricated KLH large-format plywood structure for walls and ceiling was used, and the house is anchored on two concrete supports. This structure reduces CO_2 emissions associated with foundations and structures. The facades are airy and finished with softwood.

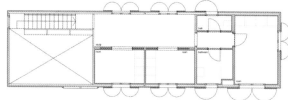

First floor plan

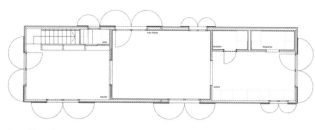

Ground floor plan

Longitudinal section

Cross section

011

Pre-existing flat areas should be used to preserve forest terrain and prevent the need for large-scale earthmoving.

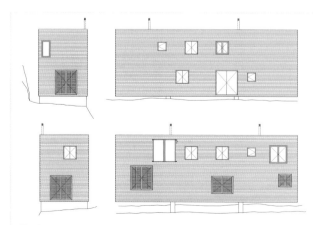

Elevations

This partly prefabricated structure provides an important reduction in weight, materials, and energy that a traditional structure, consequently resulting in lower CO_2 emissions.

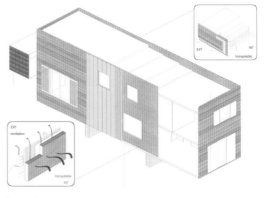

Axonometry

012

Laminated timber is a renewable material and part of a collapsible system. It is therefore reusable and recyclable, and has an almost closed life cycle.

Barn House

Architect: **Buro II**
Location: **Roeselare, Belgium**
Year of construction: **2005**
Photography: **Kris Vandamme**

Building reuse is often overshadowed by the new resources that sustainable residential architecture uses. But to give a second life to a structure, as in the case of this old barn, is an equally valuable idea when it comes to sustainability. Buro II carried out the restoration based on respect for the environment and the original concept behind the building, maintaining its original barn shape.

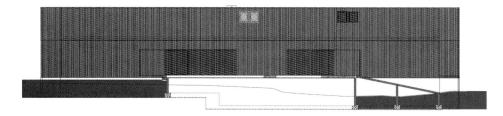

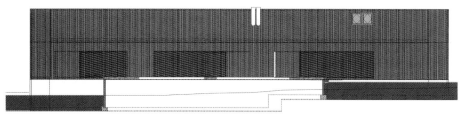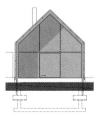

Elevations

013

The decision whether to use a gable roof or a flat roof will depend on the climate. A gable roof can elevate interior space by as much as 2.5 meters (8.5 feet) in the central area.

014

The most appropriate openings
are those facing the points
where diffuse sunlight is
captured; toward the south in
the northern hemisphere, and
toward the north in the southern
hemisphere.

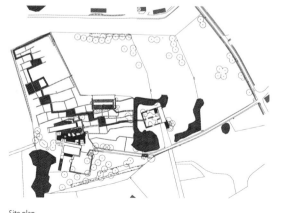

Site plan

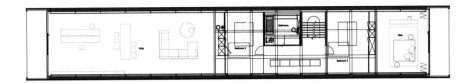

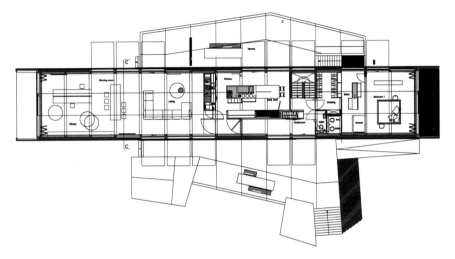

Plans

Hof Residence

Architect: Studio Granda
Location: Skagafjörður fjord,
Iceland
Year of construction: 2007
Photography: Sigurgeir
Sigurjónsson

This house is devised to endure low temperatures and to maximize natural light. The interior is thermally stable because of its concrete walls and stone floor. Geothermal water is used for underfloor heating, radiators, and domestic activities. The little electricity that is required comes from hydroelectric and geothermal sources.

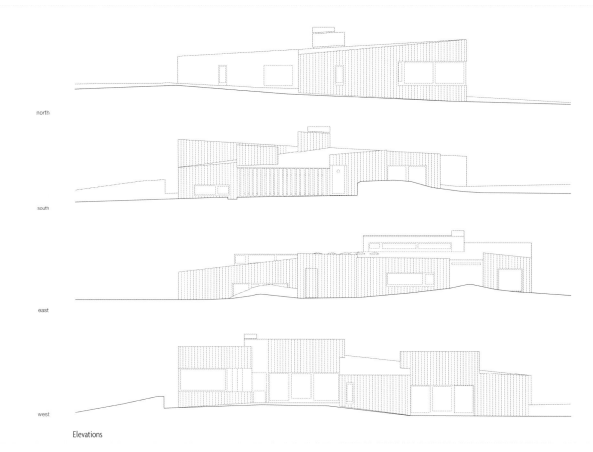

north

south

east

west

Elevations

015

Grass removed from a site during construction can be replanted on the roof. For this project, a ramp featuring grass and stone was designed to lead to the entrance of the house.

016

Almost 20 percent of energy is lost through thermal bridges. Exterior insulation, elimination of niches, and the use of flashing and compact joinery will reduce this loss.

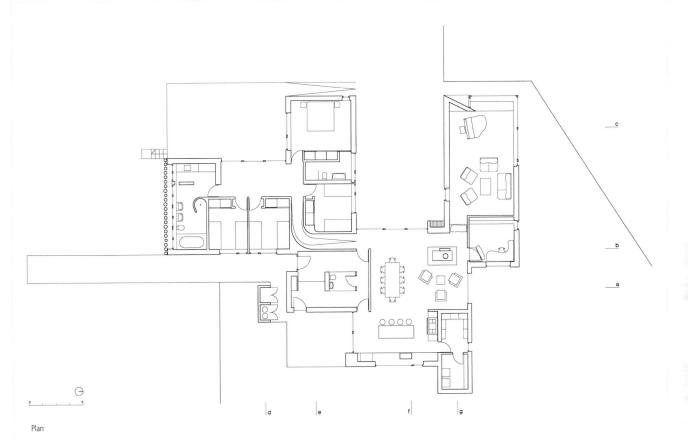

c

b

a

0   5

Plan

d   e   f   g

017

Some building materials, such as reinforced concrete, store heat and release it hours later.

Nature and architecture come together as one in House C. The roof was covered with soil and wild grass seeds, which act as thermal insulation. The same kind of soil was mixed with cement and resin for the walls, thereby reducing wall cladding and material transport costs. The color of the roof changes each season, and its appearance depends on the seeds carried by wind and birds.

House C

Architects: Hiroshi Nakamura &
NAP Architects
Location: Chiba, Japan
Year of construction: 2008
Photography: Hiroshi Nakamura
& NAP Architects

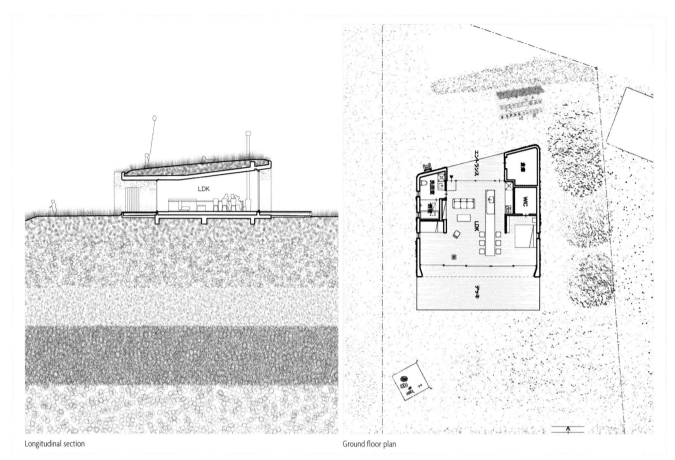

Longitudinal section

Ground floor plan

018

A flat roof receives 100 percent of the day's sun. A green roof insulates the interior at times of peak radiation.

The rammed-earth technique was done with soil sourced locally and from the actual site mixed with a small portion of concrete. The mixture was poured into the formwork and pressed.

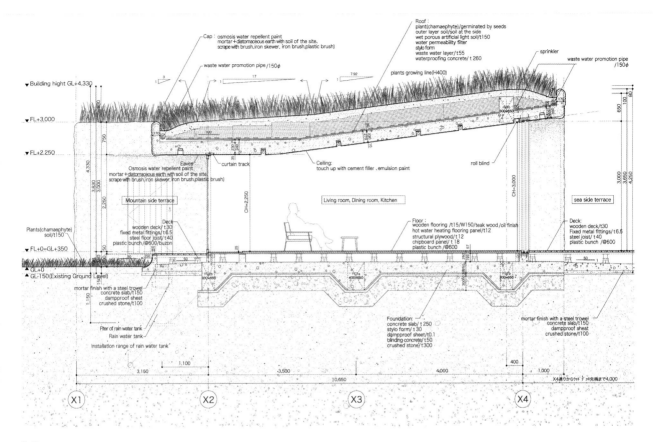

Cap : osmosis water repellent paint
mortar+diatomaceous earth with soil of the site.
scrape with brush,iron skewer, iron brush,plastic brush)

waste water promotion pipe /150φ

Roof :
plant(chamaephyte)/germinated by seeds
outer layer soil/soil at the side
wet porous artificial light soil/t150
water permeability filter
stylo form
waste water layer/ t55
waterproofing concrete/ t 260

sprinkler

waste water promotion pipe
/150φ

plants growing line(H400)

▼ Building hight GL+4,330

▼ FL+3,000

▼ FL+2,250

Eaves :
Osmosis water repellent paint
mortar + diatomaceous earth with soil of the site.
scrape with brush,iron skewer, iron brush,plastic brush)

curtain track

Ceiling :
touch up with cement filler , emulsion paint

roll blind

Mountain side terrace

Living room, Dining room, Kitchen

sea side terrace

Plants(chamaephyte)
soil/t150)

▼ FL+0=GL+350

Deck :
wooden deck/ t30
fixed metal fittings/t6.5
steel floor joist/t40
plastic bunch /@600/buzn

Floor :
wooden flooring /t15/W150/teak wood /oil finish
hot water heating flooring panel/t12
structural plywood/t12
chipboard panel/ t 18
plastic bunch /@600

Deck :
wooden deck/t30
Fixed metal fittings/t6.5
steel joist/ t40
plastic bunch /@600

▲ GL+0
▲ GL-150(Existing Ground Level)

mortar finish with a steel trowel
concrete slab/t150
dampproof sheat
crushed stone/t100

Filter of rain water tank

Rain water tank

Installation range of rain water tank

Foundation:
concrete slab/ t 250
stylo form/ t 30
dampproof sheet/t0.1
blinding concrete/t50
crushed stone/t300

mortar finish with a steel trowel
concrete slab/t150
dampproof sheat
crushed stone/t100

3,150   1,100   -3,500   4,000   1,000   400

10,650

X1   X2   X3   X4

Section

019

Interior spaces need adequate
hygrothermal conditions for
their occupants and should
always respond to climatic
conditions.

Desert Flight

Architect: Brent Kendle
Location: Scottsdale, AZ, USA
Year of construction: 2007
Photography: Rick Brazil

Located in the Arizona desert, this home uses desert soil to cover its walls, not only for their ecological benefits but also as an efficient insulation system. Its orientation, the angle of the roof and the eaves avoids excessive sun exposure during the hottest hours of the day. The roof collects rainwater for reuse in the outdoor facilities.

020

The slope of a roof and its eaves should be designed to take into account the different angles of the sun's rays in winter and summer.

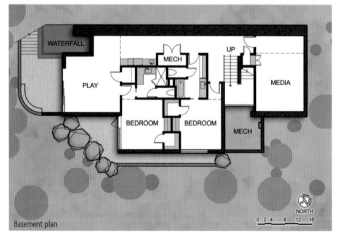

Basement plan

NORTH

0 2 4   8   12 16

021

Whether in the form of a swimming pool or a small pond, the presence of water will cool the air because it absorbs energy as it evaporates.

First level plan

Casa en Chihuahua

Architect: Carlos Bedoya, Victor Jaime, Wonne Ickx, Abel Perles/ Productora
Location: Chihuahua, Mexico
Year of construction: 2008
Photography: Iwan Baan

This project is located on land with a 20 percent slope and an extreme climate. Part of the house was buried to conserve the temperature in winter and keep the house cool in summer. The walls of the buried section were built with a double partition of concrete blocks with air chambers to thermally insulate it and prevent moisture.

EAST ELEVATION

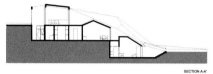

Longitudinal section

SECTION A-A'

Longitudinal section

SECTION C-C'

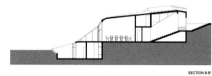

Longitudinal section

SECTION B-B'

Cross section

SECTION D-D'

Elevations   WEST ELEVATION

022

Semisunken buildings provide thermal mass for geothermal heat storage, while being protected from the wind.

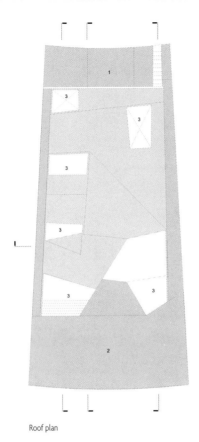

Roof plan

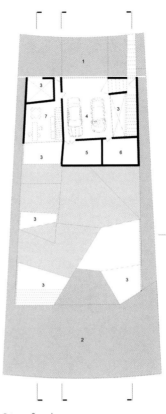

Entrance floor plan

023

The location of courtyards, terraces, and glazed expanses should be prioritized to provide views of their landscapes and to capture sunlight.

House in Moriyama

The customer's desire for this house was for it to have a bright and colorful garden. In response to this desire, Suppose Design Office designed a garden room for plants—a green room that runs throughout the interior of the house. This design stands out not just for its ability to create a natural environment inside the home but also because it created a natural interior air purifier.

Architect: Suppose Design Office
Location: Moriyama-ku, Nagoya, Japan
Year of construction: 2009
Photography: Toshiyuki Yano, Nacasa & Partners

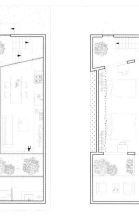

Plans

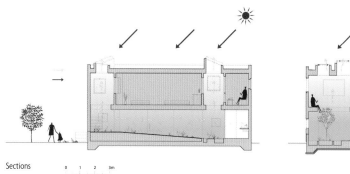

Sections

0   1   2   3m

024

The effects of natural lighting are determined by a building's orientation and its use of space-protection systems to control the entry of sunlight.

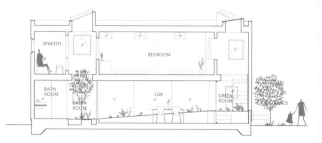

Longitudinal section

Skylights were built to allow sunlight falling on the roof into windowless spaces.

025

It is now recognized that indoor plants are able to cleanse the air and improve the chemical composition of interior environments.

House in Saijo

Architect: **Suppose Design Office**
Location: **Saijo, Hiroshima, Japan**
Year of construction: **2007**
Photography: **Toshiyuki Yano,**
Nacasa & Partners

This house developed by Suppose Design Office was built with a 3.3 feet deep semibasement created to form a protective barrier around the perimeter, while also acting as a base for the house. The surplus land from the earthwork was reused to shape the hill that acts as an outdoor garden.

Plan

Plan

Cross section

building site : Saijo,Higashihiroshima,Hiroshima,Japan
principal use : parsonal house
site area : 246m²
building area : 50.41m²
total floor area : 115.51m²

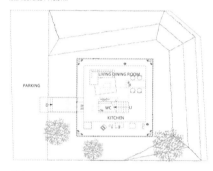

Plan

Four V-shaped steel panels were
positioned to support the weight of the
structure.

026

Upgrading old appliances
enhances energy savings.
Indiscriminate use of
dishwashers, washing machines,
and tumble dryers increases
energy consumption.

The banisterless central staircase has a
dual function: it connects the house's
different levels and it forms a volume
that occupies the core space.

027

Water use can be optimized by the correct use of sanitary fixtures. Aerators reduce water consumption by faucets.

Cabbagetown Residence

One of the main challenges during the conversion of this dwelling was to develop a new sustainable construction. It is highly insulated, with low-energy double-glazed joinery that takes advantage of the building's southern orientation to attract heat in the winter months. The floor was covered with renewable Jatoba wood.

Architect: Dubbeldam Design Architects
Location: Toronto, Canada
Year of construction: 2008
Photography: Shai Gil

028

The strategy for single- and double-height interior spaces is to use clerestory and interior windows to enhance the Venturi effect.

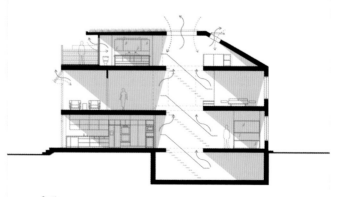

Section

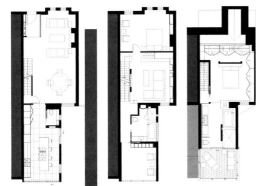

Plans

029

Cabbagetown Residence
features gray-water treatment
systems, such as decanting and
biological filters, for removing
unpleasant smells from toilets.

Marcus Beach House

The latest refurbishment work at Marcus Beach House involved the use of passive sustainability principles. Windows and doors were strategically placed to prioritize drafts, and the roof generously extends, forming eaves to protect it from sunlight. The use of artificial light was minimized, and good use is made of the natural light that enters through the windows facing north.

Architect: Bark Design Architects
Location: Queensland, Australia
Year of construction: 2009
Photography: Christopher
Frederick Jones

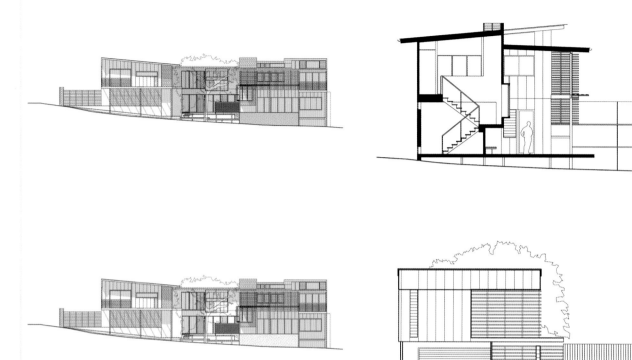

Elevations

030

The sunshades have folding guiderails and prevent sunlight from entering without blocking the view.

031

Interior gardens and courtyards improve air quality, regulate temperature, provide greenery, and encourage the preservation of biodiversity.

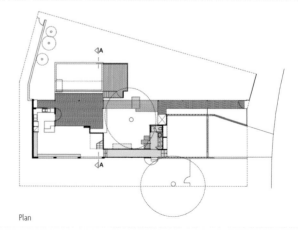

Plan

Architect: Paul McKean
Architecture
Location: Hood River, OR, USA
Year of construction: 2006
Photography: Paul McKean
Architecture

The Neal Creek Retreat owners were interested in a home that was self-sufficient. They raised it above ground level to protect it in the case of flood or fire. The green roof and structural materials are highly insulating. The house does not use fossil fuel but is fed through a hydraulic system located near the Columbia River to generate the required electricity.

The home is elevated over a concrete platform that stores heat.

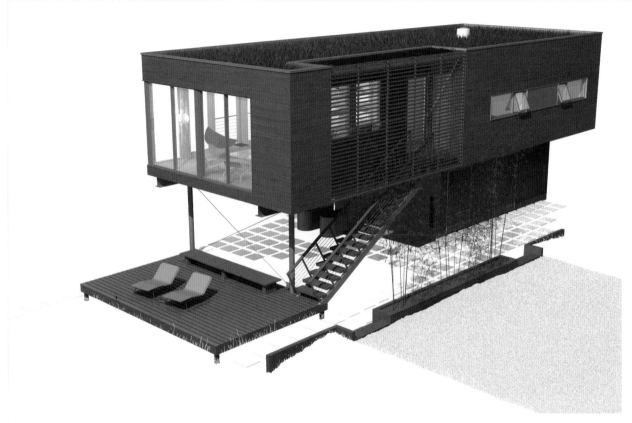

Perspective

032

Green roofs or terraces on
top of buildings are a good way
of insulating them from harsh
climatic conditions.

The owners, two windsurfing and snowboarding enthusiasts, were interested in a home that respected the surrounding greenery.

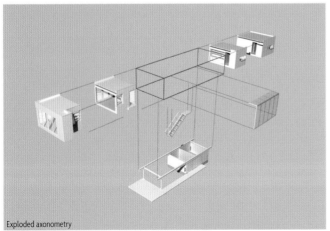

Exploded axonometry

033

Where there are very extreme climatic conditions (below 32 °F or above 91 °F), bioarchitecture recommends the use of mixed heating and cooling systems.

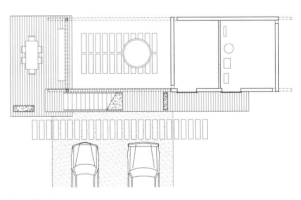

Ground floor plan

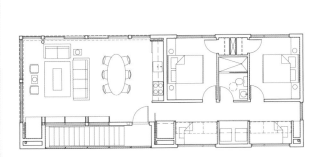

First floor plan

Maurer House

During construction of this house, the landscape was not changed. The architects took into consideration the local climate and ecosystem. Green construction materials are paramount and reduce energy consumption. Overlooking Lake Okanagan, it utilizes the environment while ensuring minimal impact.

Architect: **Florian Maurer/
Allen + Maurer Architects Ltd.**
Location: Naramata, Canada
Year of construction: 2004
Photography: Florian Maurer,
Stuart Bish

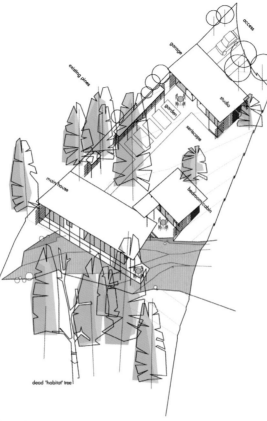

existing pines

garage

access

studio

garden

senscape

main house

bedroom/cabin

dead 'habitat' tree

Axonometry

The site features four buildings
surrounded by trees. The roofs have
simple lines and are slightly raised to
provide views of Lake Okanagan.

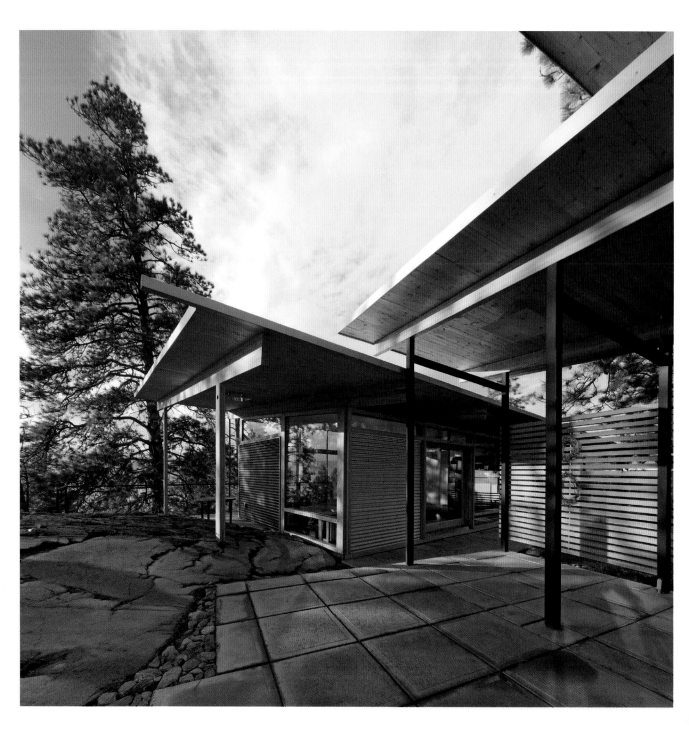

034

Among the most
environmentally friendly
materials are wood and bamboo.
On this building, they are treated
in different ways: no varnishes
or only environmentally friendly
varnishes were used.

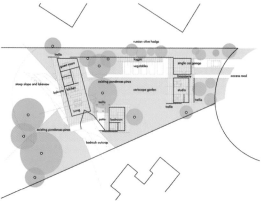

Site plan

The local vegetation was preserved—no trees were cut down and no stones were moved so as not to alter or destroy the ecosystem.

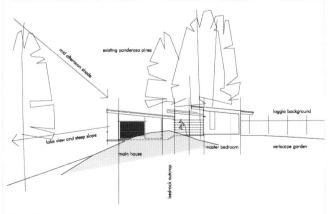

existing ponderosa pines

mid afternoon shade

loggia background

lake view and steep slope

main house

master bedroom

xeriscape garden

bedrock outcrop

Site section

035

Composting is a good solution for transforming the organic waste we produce into natural fertilizers. 220 pounds of organic waste produces 66 pounds of free fertilizer.

Ballandean House

Architect: Arkhefield
Location: Ballandean,
Queensland, Australia
Year of construction: 2006
Photography: Scott Burrows

Situated in an area of vineyards, Ballandean House stands out for the shape of its structure, which provides permanent shade thanks to the eaves that extend from the roof. The strength and soundness of the rooftop are a response to the harsh climate and landscape. There are external and underground water tanks to collect water from the roof.

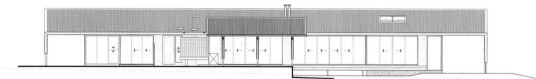

North elevation

South elevation

036

Rainwater tank size depends on the rainfall in the area and household needs.

East elevation

037

Skylights and roof-ventilation systems used as passive control strategies are traditional tools in areas of warm climate.

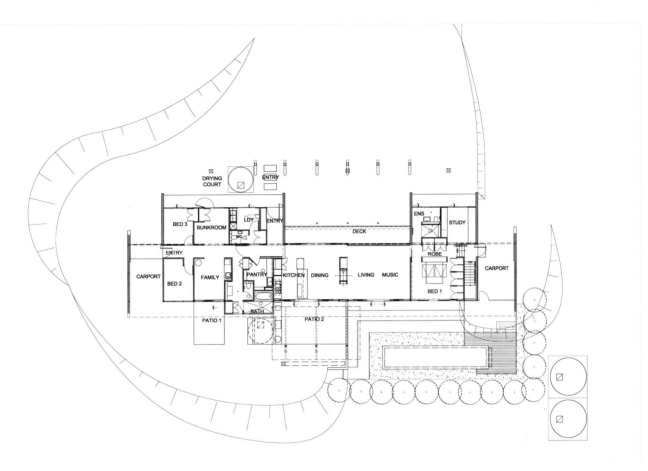

DRYING
COURT

ENTRY

BED 3

BUNKROOM

LDY

ENTRY

WC

ENS

STUDY

DECK

ROBE

ENTRY

CARPORT

BED 2

FAMILY

PANTRY

KITCHEN

DINING

LIVING

MUSIC

BED 1

CARPORT

BATH

PATIO 1

PATIO 2

The elongated floor plan enables the
living area to benefit from panoramic
views of the surrounding landscape.

Casa MC1

This contemporary tropical-style project makes use of natural resources as well as integrating and taking full advantage of the local climate. The house is oriented to take advantage of cross-ventilation and sunlight, and to achieve minimum energy consumption. It also collects rainwater for reuse in the home.

Architect: Juan Robles, Andrea Solano, Emilio Quirós/Robles Arquitectos
Location: Quepos, Costa Rica
Year of construction: 2007
Photography: Robles Arquitectos

038

The choice of a pond to absorb ambient temperature is a traditional design solution, but it enables active energy systems to be partly or fully ruled out.

The greenery and light that envelop the bedroom are an invitation to relaxation. The awnings can be lowered at dusk or when the heat is greatest.

039

After simple treatment, gray water can be reused in toilets, doing away with the need to use drinking water where it is not essential.

Love House

Love House is a building with a facade of 8.8 x 30 feet. Because of its open roof, the house has direct contact with natural light and therefore minimizes energy consumption. At night, candles are lit and artificial light is disregarded. The curved ceiling opens and the starry sky can be seen.

Architect: Takeshi Hosaka/
Takeshi Hosaka Architects
Location: Yokohama, Japan
Year of construction: 2005
Photography: Masao Nishikawa,
Koji Fujii/Nacasa & Partners

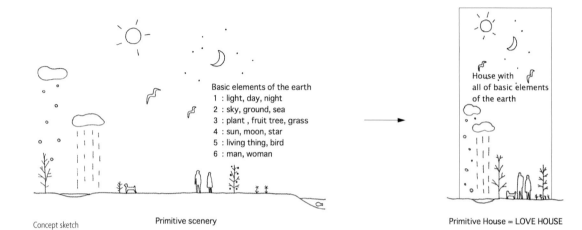

Basic elements of the earth
1 : light, day, night
2 : sky, ground, sea
3 : plant , fruit tree, grass
4 : sun, moon, star
5 : living thing, bird
6 : man, woman

House with
all of basic elements
of the earth

Concept sketch

Primitive scenery

Primitive House = LOVE HOUSE

040

Respect for the environment, with consideration for all of its components—water, soil, wildlife, landscape, and social and cultural aspects—is one of the pillars of sustainability.

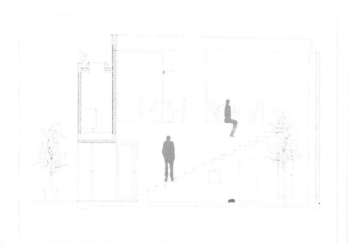

041

Reducing the use of electricity and air-conditioning is possible if openings are made in a facade to let daylight and breezes in.

The partly open roof provides visual continuity with the building's exterior and permanent contact with natural light.

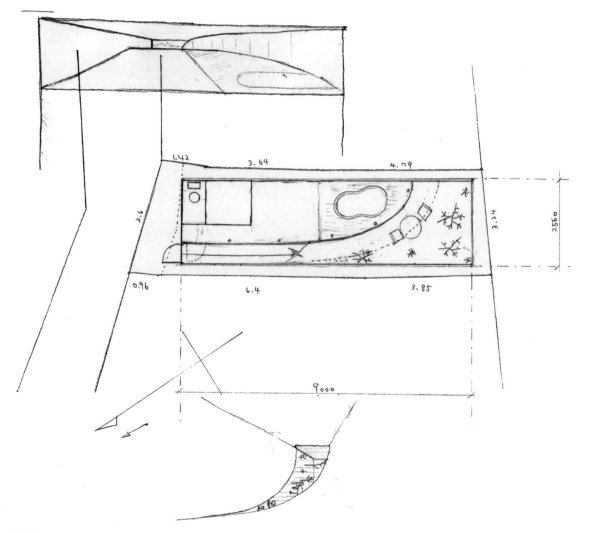

1.42   3.64   4.79

2.6   3.14

2560

0.96   6.4   3.85

9000

Sketch

900 900 900   900 900 900   900 900 900

1 F PLAN S=1/50   2 F PLAN S=1/50   ROOF S=1/50

The home has a floor space of only 355 square feet. The roof becomes the focal point for the layout of the rooms in the house.

Farmhouse Voges Redux

This renovation project is an example of the recovery of domestic vernacular architecture. Its structural shell is made of wood. The main requirements: increased presence of natural light and, therefore, increased energy efficiency. Triple-glazed joinery with thermal breaks was used to cover the porch, preventing the entry of wind and rain.

Architect: Despang Architekten
Location: Wennigsen, Germany
Year of construction: 2008
Photography: Despang
Architekten

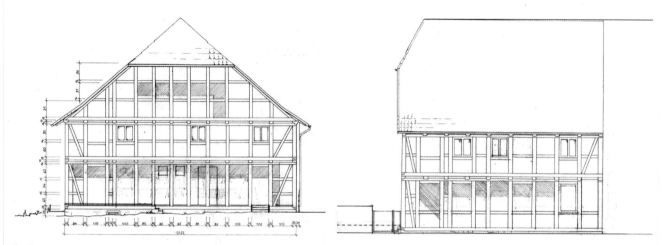

Elevations

042

Salvaged materials such as timber, which can serve as beams in a new house, are natural materials that can be given a second life.

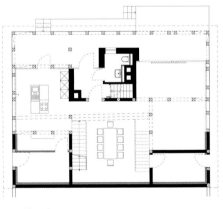

Ground floor plan

The larger windows are reserved
for the public areas and take great
advantage of daylight.

043

Materials with a low energy cost, such as certified wood and recycled metal, should be favored.

Perspective

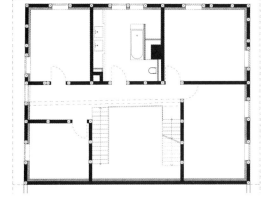

First floor plan

Della Torre House

Architect: Max Pritchard
Architect
Location: Kangarilla, Australia
Year of construction: 2008
Photography: Ben Della Torre

All rooms of this house face north to enjoy the winter sun. The roof, which extends over the house like a parasol, favors sun exposure in winter and allows cross-ventilation in summer. The concrete floor and double-glazed joinery maintain the temperature indoors. Rainwater is collected to water the garden.

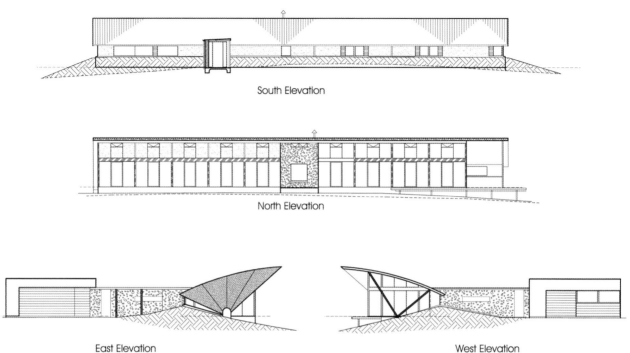

South Elevation

North Elevation

East Elevation

West Elevation

Elevations

044

Dirt and excess heat are factors that can alter the quality of water stored in tanks. They should be protected against.

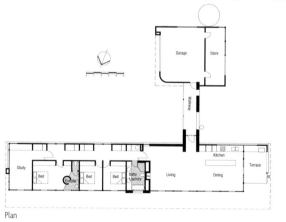

Plan

045

Electronic pellet-burning stoves
and solar thermal panels
are an ideal combination for
heating from an economic and
ecological point of view.

Villa G

Todd Saunders has managed to combine traditional building materials from local sources such as wood paneling with high-design concepts and achieve a low environmental impact. This house is distinguished by expanses of glass on the first floor, offering magnificent views of the dunes. Given its location in a windy area, Villa G maximizes any possibility of harnessing the sun.

Architect: Saunders Architecture
Location: Hjellestad, Bergen, Norway
Year of construction: 2009
Photography: Bent René Synnvåg, Jan Lillebø

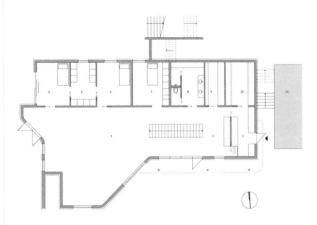

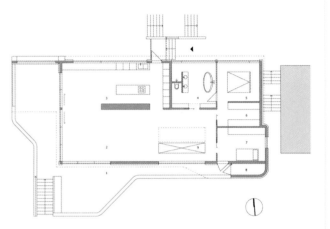

Plans

046

Laminated timber is a renewable
material and part of a collapsible
system. It is therefore reusable
and recyclable, and has a
practically closed life cycle.

047

Glazed walls do away with the need for artificial lighting during the day by letting natural light into the least endowed spaces.

Milly Film

Architect: Philippe Samyn and
Partners
Location: Inkebeek, Belgium
Year of construction: 2007
Photography: Marie-Françoise
Plissart

The house and studio of a cinema maker, Milly Film is characterized by the green facade on its north, east, and south sides, which contrast with the fully glazed west facade. It features good insulation, irrigation systems, and fertilization systems. Its vegetation includes exotic plants chosen by botanist Patrick Blanc and planted on rigid PVC panels.

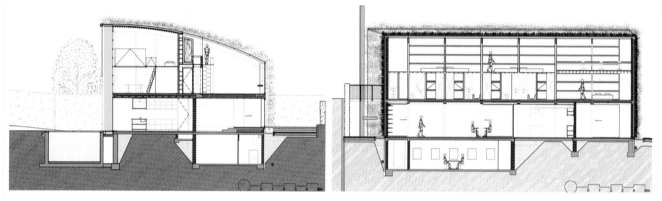

Sections

Glazed openings prevent the escape of
heat from materials that store it for later
release, such as concrete.

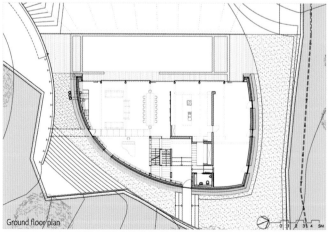

Ground floor plan

0 1 2 3 4 5M

048

Heavy building materials generally act as effective thermal mass. Their effectiveness is increased when they are strategically located to receive solar radiation through glass.

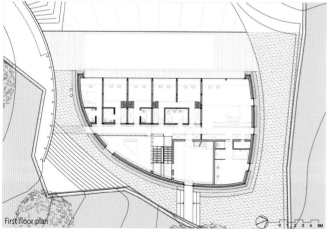

First floor plan

0 1 2 3 4 5M

Aloni

Architect: decaARCHITECTURE
Location: Antiparos Island,
Greece
Year of construction: 2008
Photography: Erietta Attali, Ed
Reeve, Julia Klimi,
decaARCHITECTURE

decaARCHITECTURE took advantage of the slope of two mountains to create this spectacular home adapted to the topography of the area. The building is almost hidden underground and merges with the environment. The outdoor patios and white walls make it obvious that this is a house, and the terraces, which are also roofs in some cases, are covered with the same vegetation. The lighting is completely natural.

049

Sinking a building brings the benefits of permanent and stored heat in the ground in winter and thermal inertia for cooling in summer.

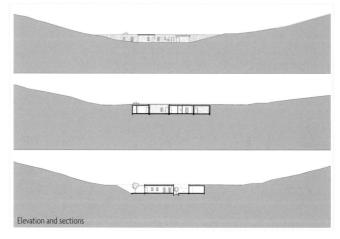

Elevation and sections

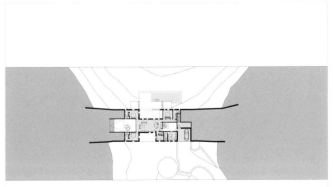

Plan

050

The greatest benefits of a green roof are rainwater management, lower energy costs, and its contribution to soundproofing.

Glasshouse

Located on Stoney Lake, gh3 used the environment as a design element for this house by opening up the facade 360 degrees. The structure takes advantage of the thermal mass of granite to avoid using active systems in winter. The glass facade has movable panels that provide natural ventilation while a system of automatic blinds, the white roof, and a fence protect the house from the excessive heat.

Architect: gh3
Location: Stoney Lake, Ontario, Canada
Year of construction: 2008
Photography: Larry Williams

East elevation

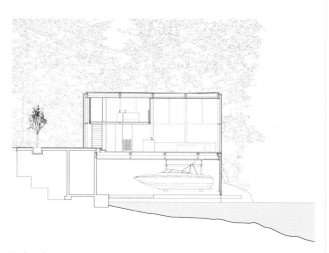

North-south section

This house is situated between rocks and on the water's edge. The roof is flat to reduce its visual impact on the lake.

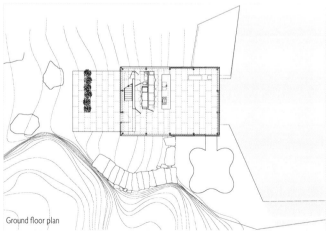

Ground floor plan

051

Research is being done on photochromatic materials that respond to changes in light and on multilayer panels that respond by changing their color or opacity.

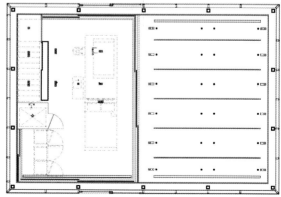

Reflected ceiling plan

052

There are experiments being performed on panels containing chemical liquids or gases that provide insulation and heat storage.

House in Colina

Architect: Felipe del Río,
Federico Campino/OPA
Location: Colina, Chile
Year of construction: 2009
Photography: Nico Saieh,
Cristina Alemparte

The formal concept for this home was a reinterpretation of traditional rustic buildings. The sheer size of the house causes heating and energy issues. As a strategy, an insulating perimeter wall was used for increased thermal capacity. A cross-ventilation system was created to foster the cross-current flow and passive extraction of hot air.

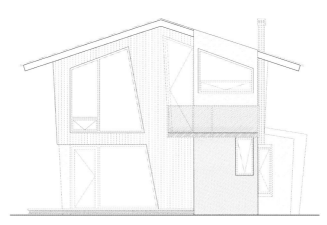

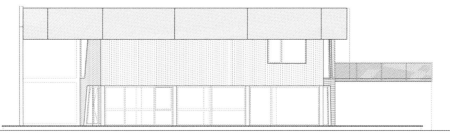

Elevations

053

Natural cross-ventilation loses its practical significance in winter, a time when warm, heated air is lost, and only one part of a house can be ventilated.

054

Reinforced concrete buildings have between 10 and 20 percent lower building costs and guarantee up to an 80 percent reduction in heating costs.

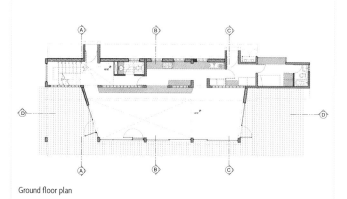

Ground floor plan

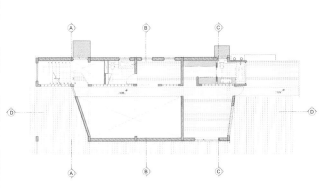

First floor plan

Narrabeen House

Architect: Choi Ropiha
Location: Narrabeen, Australia
Year of construction: 2009
Photography: Simon Whitbread,
Choi Ropiha

This house is situated beside Lake Narrabeen with views of the lake and casuarina vegetation. Its designers considered weather conditions, hydrography, and the ecosystem to create a building with maximum performance but minimal impact. The house stands 4 feet above the average water level for protection in case of flooding.

Drip irrigation systems and timers can be
installed in gardens to avoid excess waste.

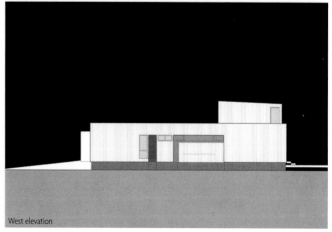

West elevation

055

The building industry is responsible for 40 percent of CO_2 emissions. Using locally sourced materials reduces a building's carbon footprint and encourages the development of local industry.

056

Courtyards enhance air flow in winter, meaning that it is not necessary to ventilate the entire house when ventilating only a part is sufficient.

Public spaces are laid out around
the courtyard and are permanently
ventilated.

Montecito Residence

Architect: Olson Kundig
Architects
Location: Toro Canyon, CA, USA
Year of construction: 2008
Photography: Jim Bartsch, Tim
Bies, Nikolas Koenig

Montecito Residence is a single-family house located in an area prone to fires. The owners wanted to minimize the use of scarce natural resources. The roof collects rain water in a deposit, which can also be used in the case of a fire. The roof has eaves to prevent direct radiation. Fire-resistant materials were specially selected.

1. Cross ventilation through both axis
2. Dutch door controls air flow
3. Pool cools wind through evaporation
4. Roof overhang (and double roof construction) protects against direct sun and reduces heat gain
5. Overhead perforated rolling shutters protects against direct sun, severe wind, and possible fire while preserving views
6. All exterior materials are non-combustible
7. Originally designed with a cistern to collect rain water for irrigation

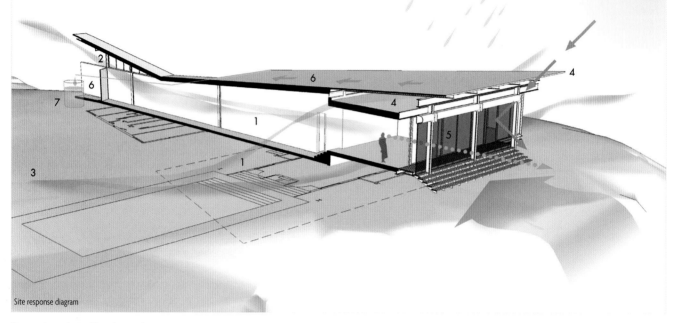

Site response diagram

Breezes in contact with water produce
evaporation that lowers air temperature.

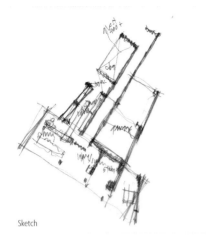

Sketch

057

Operable windows, hatches
in doors, and roofs create
ventilation systems.

058

Evaporation-based or bioclimatic heating and cooling systems are effective because they only need water, which is returned to the atmosphere as water vapor, to function.

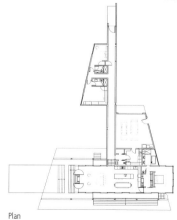

Plan

Centrifugal Villa

Centrifugal Villa is organized around a hollow center, as if the heart of the house had somehow fallen outside its body. The experience of the interior is characterized by constantly shifting vanishing points, with large openings in the roof and vertical walls that allow a view of the surrounding landscape. The outer cladding is characterized by crossed wooden slats to ensure natural ventilation.

Architect: OBRA Architects
Location: Southampton, NY, USA
Year of construction: 2008
Photography: OBRA Architects

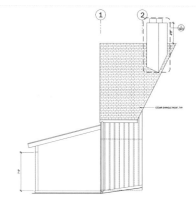

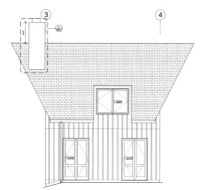

Elevation

The timber-plank latticework structure offers views of the nearby agricultural reserve.

059

Air-conditioning may be unnecessary if the orientation of a house is combined with windows, doors, and balconies designed to take advantage of breezes.

Transversal section

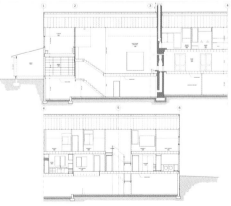

Longitudinal section

Ground floor plan

Second floor plan

Active Energy Strategies

Mountain Research

Architect: Shin Ohori, Setaro Aso/General Design
Location: Kawakami-mura, Nagano, Japan
Year of construction: 2008
Photography: Daici Ano

Local pine wood from the mountains at Kawakami-mura is the main material used in this vacation home. The house uses the energy provided by solar panels, which convert solar radiation into electricity. The different rooms are arranged to maximize the daylight hours and to enhance scenic views.

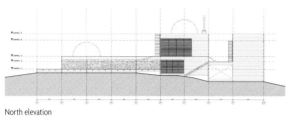

North elevation

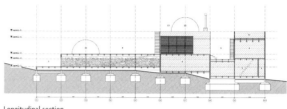

Longitudinal section

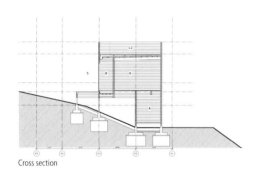

Cross section

060

In places that are heavily wooded or have thick undergrowth, reducing the impact on the terrain means building on platforms.

Homes can function as single large spaces or as a series of well-connected private spaces.

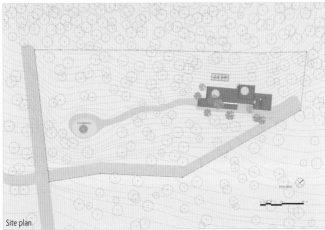

Site plan

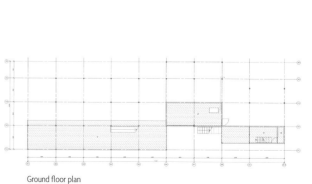

Ground floor plan

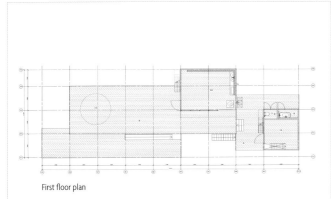

First floor plan

061

Water-conserving fixtures,
for example dual-flush toilets,
contribute to efficient water use
and keep expenses low.

40 Homes for Young People

This social housing project is based on five sustainable points: natural ventilation, thermal insulation in walls and roofs, gray-water recycling for irrigation use, application of materials and industrialized construction systems, and the reducing of waste production on site. A solar panel for heating water was installed in each home.

Architect: Miguel Arraiz García, Bruno Sauer/Bipolaire Arquitectos
Location: Torrevieja, Spain
Year of construction: 2006
Photography: Noel Arraiz

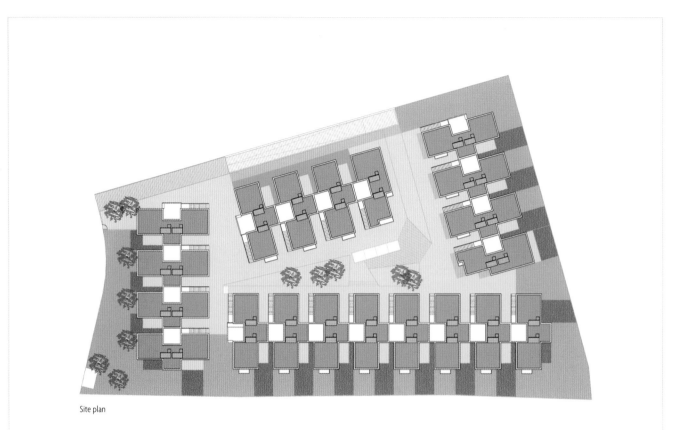

Site plan

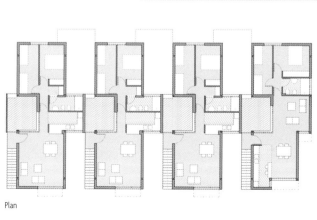

Plan

062

Poor insulation can lead to a large amount of energy being wasted. Airtight joinery will ensure internal thermal efficency.

Each block contains eight or sixteen housing units. The comb-like design was chosen to create private courtyards and enhance cross-ventilation.

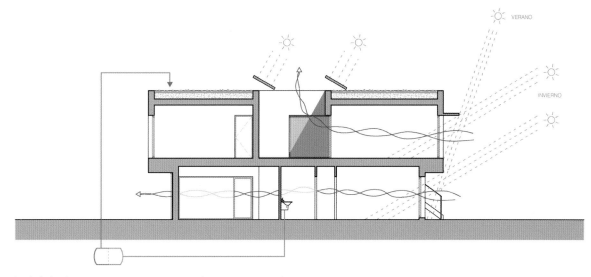

Longitudinal section

063

High-efficiency lighting enables a building to consume less energy. Its intensity can be regulated as needed.

Brooks Avenue House

Built as an extension of the main dwelling, the new volume of this building is clad with indigenous, low-maintenance grasses and shrubs. Recycled rainwater is used to irrigate the vegetation and for domestic use. The house has a high-efficiency boiler that supplies hot water for underfloor heating. The finishes are low in volatile organic compounds.

Architect: Bricault Design
Location: Venice, CA, USA
Year of construction: 2009
Photography: Kenji Arai, Danna Kinsky

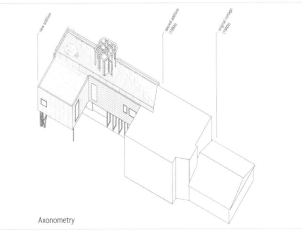

Axonometry

064

Green roofs featuring drought-resistant native species reduce the effects of overheating.

Ground level

Second level

Roof level

Plans

065

Renewed air is essential to maintain good conditions for interior comfort.

Northbeach Residence

Located in an area of archaeological interest, Northbeach's artificially created foundations were minimized to ensure a low environmental and visual impact. The green roof has filters that collect rainwater for irrigation. The hot water supply and hydronic heating is provided by thermal solar panels on the roof, while an additional photovoltaic solar panel, located under the green roof, provides electricity.

Architect: Heliotrope
Location: Orcas Island, WA, USA
Year of construction: 2009
Photography: Benjamin Benschneider

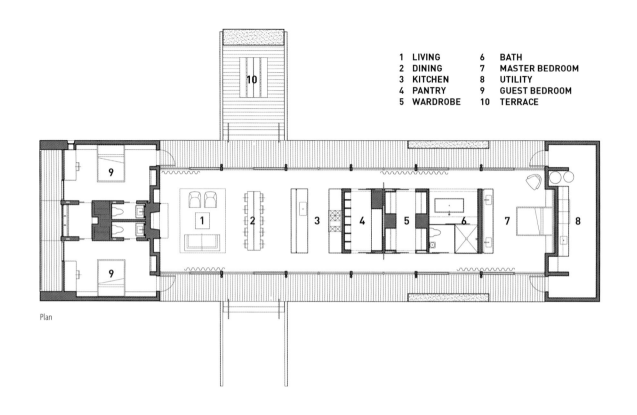

1	LIVING	6	BATH
2	DINING	7	MASTER BEDROOM
3	KITCHEN	8	UTILITY
4	PANTRY	9	GUEST BEDROOM
5	WARDROBE	10	TERRACE

Plan

066

In warm climates with plentiful sunlight, a green roof and climbing plants on walls create energy savings.

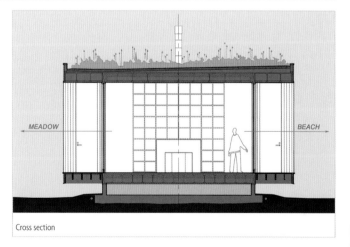

Cross section

MEADOW

BEACH

The kitchen receives natural daylight and the home is well ventilated.

067

Passive heating and cooling systems are more effective when there is a separate control that only enables conventional systems if necessary.

Yoga Studio

This small structure combines a yoga studio and a guesthouse. The studio has an integrated geothermal system that provides efficient heating and cooling systems to meet the studio's hot water needs. Passive systems with large windows were chosen to maximize light. The green rooftop and use of sustainable materials are outstanding features.

Architect: Carter + Burton
Architecture, PLC.
Location: Clarke County, VA, USA
Year of construction: 2007
Photography: Carter + Burton
Architecture, PLC.

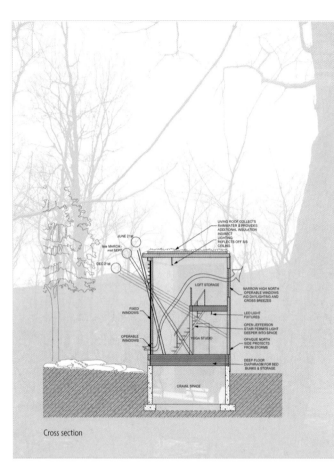

LIVING ROOF COLLECTS
RAINWATER & PROVIDES
ADDITIONAL INSULATION
INDIRECT
LIGHTING
REFLECTS OFF S/S
CEILING

JUNE 21st

New MARCH–
mid SEPT

DEC 21st

LOFT STORAGE

NARROW HIGH NORTH
OPERABLE WINDOWS
AID DAYLIGHTING AND
CROSS BREEZES

FIXED
WINDOWS

LED LIGHT
FIXTURES

OPEN JEFFERSON
STAIR PERMITS LIGHT
DEEPER INTO SPACE

OPERABLE
WINDOWS

YOGA STUDIO

OPAQUE NORTH
SIDE PROTECTS
FROM STORMS

DEEP FLOOR
DIAPHRAGM FOR BED
BUNKS & STORAGE

CRAWL SPACE

Cross section

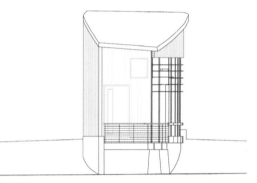

East Elevation

West Elevation

Elevations

068

Windows need to be on
opposing sides for a ventilation
system to be effective. Their
interior frames should encourage
cross-ventilation.

069

The two associations guaranteeing the controlled origin of wood are the Forest Stewardship Council (FSC) and the Pan European Forest Council (PEFC).

Mattresses for resting and yoga are
stored under the floor by means of a
system of folding hatches.

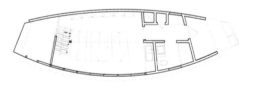

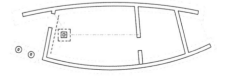

Air House

Architect: François Perrin
Location: Brentwood, CA, USA
Year of construction: 2007
Photography: Michael Wells,
Joshua White

Air House stands out for its wooden structure covered with a polycarbonate second skin. This system creates an air chamber between the wood and plastic surfaces of its structure that acts as thermal protection due to the greenhouse effect. Energy is supplied by solar panels on the roof and by wind turbines. The orientation of the house benefits from air currents that cool the interior.

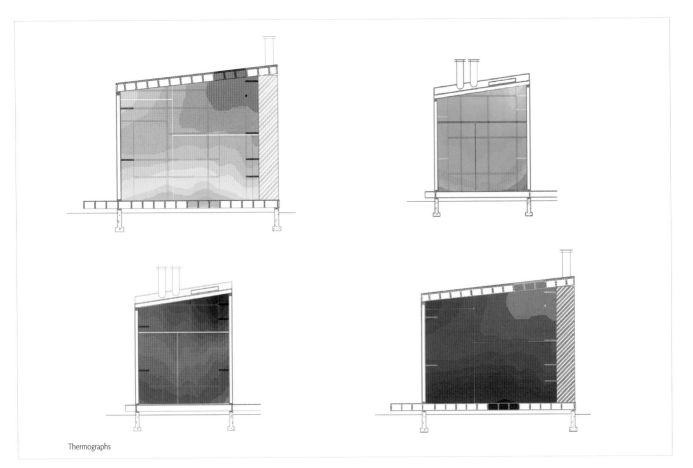

Thermographs

Diagram showing energy peaks during
the seasonal cycle.

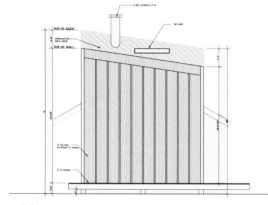

North elevation

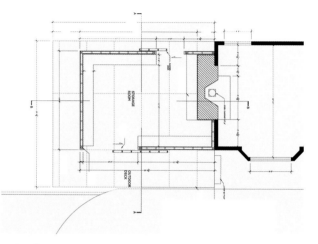

First floor plan

070

Energy-capturing systems can be optimized through the use of glass-enclosed balconies, which produce a greenhouse effect.

071

While the use of natural lighting is an energy-saving measure, it also creates a warm and friendly interior ambiance.

Bluff House

The shell of this house is composed of polyurethane structural insulated panels (SIPs) in the walls and ceiling, and the low-emission windows contain argon for insulation. The main level features a hydronic radiant floor heating system to maintain a comfortable atmosphere. Outside air is filtered through a fan that purifies it without cooling the room's temperature.

Architect: Bruns Architecture
Location: Baraboo, WI, USA
Year of construction: 2009
Photography: Bruns Architecture

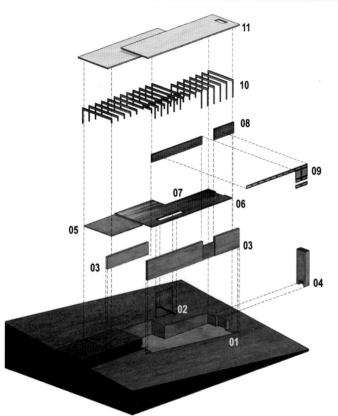

11

10

08

09

07

06

05

03

03

04

02

01

Axonometry

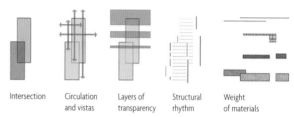

Intersection

Circulation and vistas

Layers of transparency

Structural rhythm

Weight of materials

Diagrams

072

Interstitial condensation represents an obvious loss of the insulating quality of materials. To counter this, the use of balanced insulation materials, like expanded polystyrene or expanded glass, is recommended.

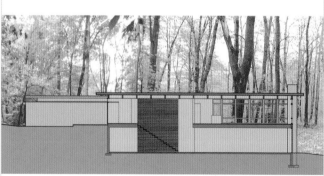

Longitudinal section

Floor plan

01 Entry walk
02 Entry
03 Circulation hall
04 Kitchen
05 Dining room
06 Living room
07 Bedroom
08 Walk-in closet
09 Bath
10 Garage
11 Deck
12 Mechanical
13 Laundry

0   10   20

Plans

073

The building's appliance that currently uses the most energy is the refrigerator. Highly insulated refrigerators reduce energy loss when closed.

Clay Field

Clay Field is a group of twenty-six affordable and sustainable homes. The buildings make use of a spray made from a blend of hemp and lime that captures carbon from the atmosphere. A biomass heating system heats the house from a boiler. The construction combines contemporary design and energy efficiency, using local materials where possible.

Architect: Riches Hawley
Mikhail Architects
Location: Elmswell, Suffolk, UK
Year of construction: 2008
Photography: Tim Crocker,
Nick Kane

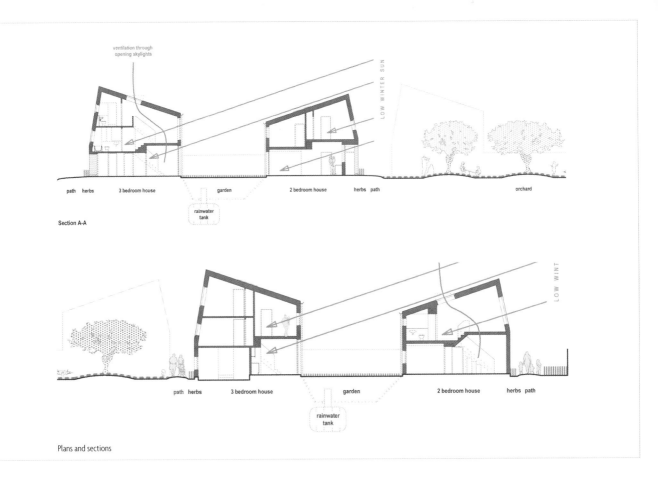

ventilation through
opening skylights

LOW WINTER SUN

path   herbs   3 bedroom house   garden   2 bedroom house   herbs path   orchard

rainwater
tank

Section A-A

LOW WINT

path herbs   3 bedroom house   garden   2 bedroom house   herbs path

rainwater
tank

Plans and sections

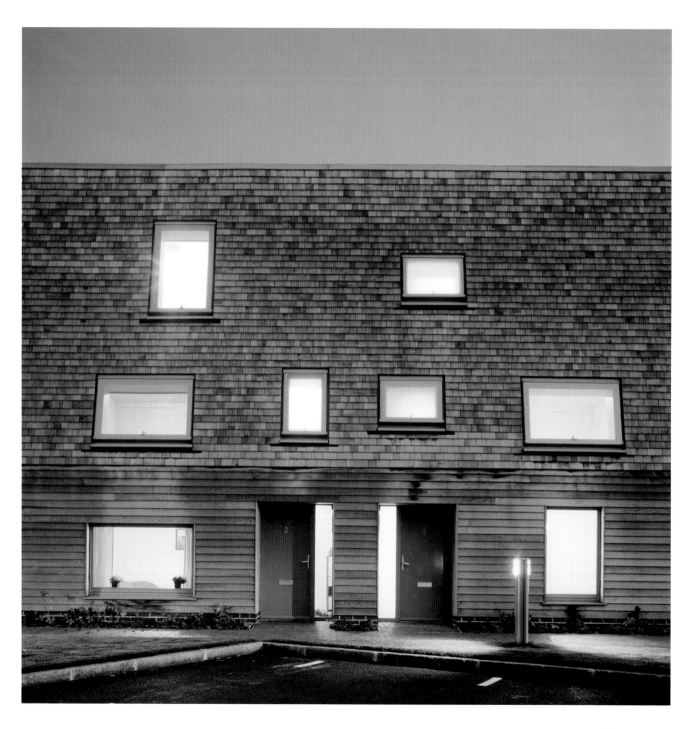

074

Once used, household water becomes sewage or gray water. Treatment enables it to be usable for watering.

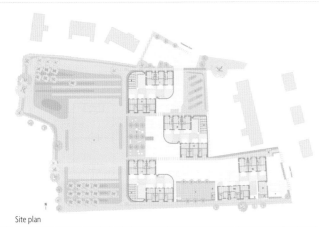

Site plan

Putney Mountain House

Architect: Kyu Sung Woo
Architects
Location: Putney, Vermont, USA
Year of construction: 2008
Photography: Kyu Sung Woo
Architects

Situated on the southwestern slope of Putney Mountain, this off-the-grid house is completely disconnected from the building's main electricity network. Its energy is supplied by photovoltaic panels. The thick walls insulate the interior in winter. A wood stove, in which the remains of locally-sourced trees are burned, is its source of heat. There is also underfloor flooring.

075

Properties that only use clean
electric power are known as
"off-the-grid" homes. They are
powered by means of active
and passive strategies.

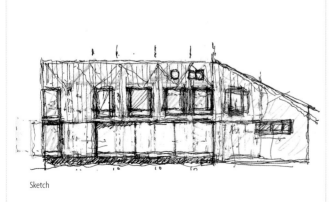

Sketch

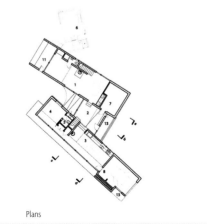

Plans

076

In places with direct sunlight, the effects of glare should be expected and prepared for.

Deepstone

During the design phase, it was decided that this dwelling should be self-sufficient. Its air filtration is minimal due to the insulation of the shell. It has triple-glazed joinery with thermal breaks. The heating is powered by a geothermal system, and there are photovoltaic solar panels to generate electricity.

Architect: Simon Winstanley Architects
Location: Solway Coast, UK
Year of construction: 2009
Photography: Simon Winstanley Architects

077

A bioclimatic house designed for heat in winter should have its main facade facing the areas that are most exposed to the sun.

Front view

Small windows afford views of the hillside in the rear of the house. Glazed expanses and the balcony face the sea to capture sunlight.

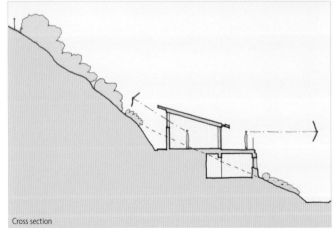

Cross section

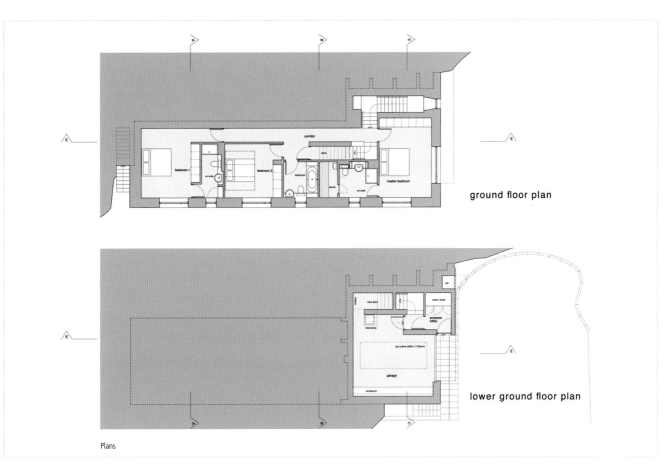

ground floor plan

lower ground floor plan

Plans

078

The most common heating
systems involve boilers.
The most effective are
low-temperature systems
and condensing boilers.

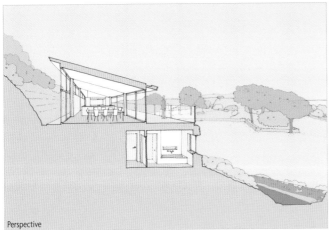

Perspective

Mackilston House

The objective of this project's architects was to build a house on one level with minimum impact to the landscape, utilizing sustainable construction, and to ensure zero CO_2 emissions for all energy use. The house boasts high levels of insulation, minimal air filtering, solar panels on the roof, and an electricity generator powered by an air turbine.

Architect: Simon Winstanley Architects
Location: Dalry, UK
Year of construction: 2009
Photography: Simon Winstanley Architects

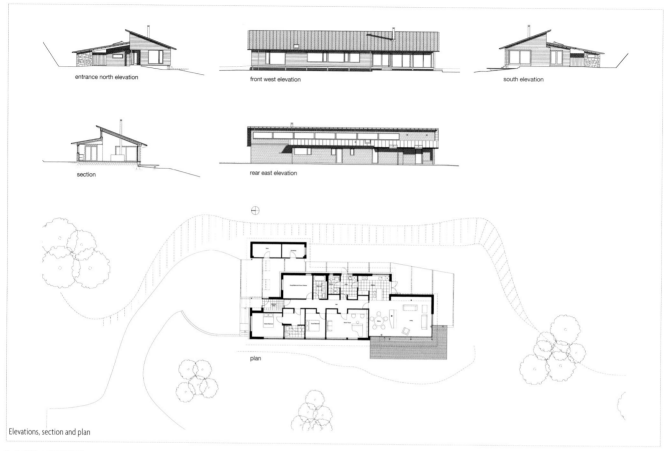

entrance north elevation

front west elevation

south elevation

section

rear east elevation

plan

Elevations, section and plan

079

Ideal materials are those with low CO_2 emissions throughout their life cycles: raw material extraction, transport, manufacturing processes, use, reuse, recycling, and final disposal.

080

Micro-wind turbines are an effective way of supplying energy for household use in places off the grid.

Casa Torcida

Casa Torcida was designed to be totally self-sufficient. The energy comes from photovoltaic cells located on the roof, complemented by a hydroelectric plant. A system for rainwater collection provides all drinking and gray water. The cross-ventilation and efficient solar-protection systems were maximized to combat the tropical climate.

Architects: Eric Gartner, Coty Sidnam/SPG Architects
Location: Osa Peninsula, Costa Rica
Year of construction: 2009
Photography: Charles Lindsay

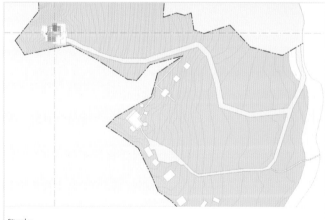

Site plan

081

Flat solar panels should be used to collect hot water for heating and household use.

082

Photovoltaic panels or small
wind turbines should be
used to produce electricity.

East elevation

Plan

The bedroom area opens to one of the terraces to provide cooling on warm nights.

H House

Group 41 created a series of active and passive strategies to ensure low energy consumption through H House. Thermal solar panels provide hot water for domestic use. The main family area and bathroom have underfloor heating. Surplus materials were reused from the demolition of a building.

Architect: Group 41
Location: Noe Valley, CA, USA
Year of construction: 2009
Photography: Eric Rorer, Ken Gutmaker

083

Radiant systems, such as underfloor, skirting-board, and wall-panel heating, consume less energy and distribute heat evenly.

084

A light meter can indicate when to open window shades and when artificial lighting should be used.

A terrace provides an outdoor living space that is ideal for entertaining.

Sandhill Pavilions

This holiday home consists of three pavilions connected by a wooden pathway. A platform located around the highest pavilion enables a view of the nearby sea. The architects saw to it that despite the home's construction, the natural environment was preserved and there was no adverse affect on the native vegetation. The home subsists on solar energy and its open spaces allow for cross-ventilation. A combustion efficiency heater regulates temperature.

Architect: Max Pritchard
Architect
Location: Island Beach, Kangaroo
Island, Australia
Year of construction: 2008
Photography: Sam Noonan

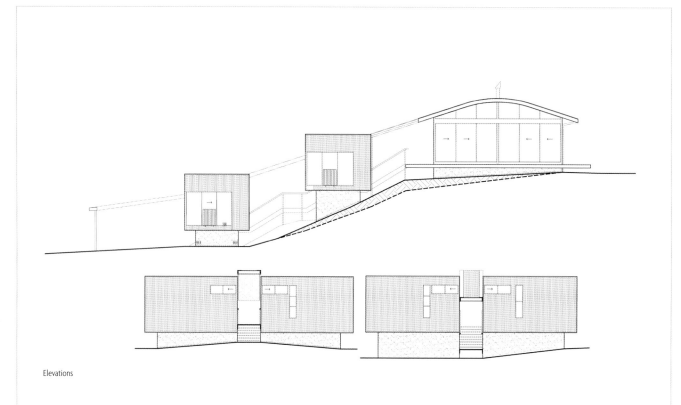

Elevations

085

One way of preventing
the destruction of wildlife
communities and ecosystems
on-site is to build on platforms
raised a few inches above the
ground.

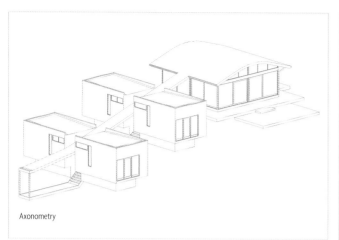

Axonometry

There is a view from the inside of the
timber deck raised over the dunes.

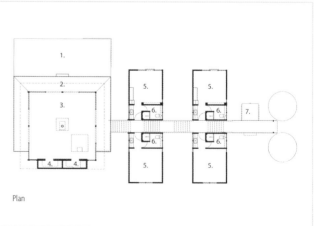

Plan

086

The most effective biomass energy systems in residential architecture are those involving natural biomass in wood- or pellet-burning stoves.

West Basin House

West Basin House can be seen as completely self-sufficient and off the grid. Its areas are divided into three volumes connected through porches that lead to the courtyard. Traditional building systems were chosen such as rammed earth, in which crude stone as well as concrete were used. Some thirty-six external panels and two fixed thermal solar panels on the roof handle the heating and electricity requirements.

Architect: Signer Harris Architects
Location: Galisteo Basin Reserve, Santa Fe, NM, USA
Year of construction: 2007
Photography: Kirk Gittings

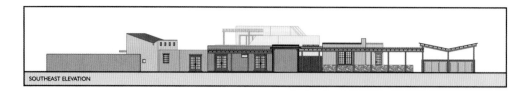

SOUTHEAST ELEVATION

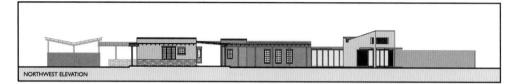

NORTHWEST ELEVATION

NORTHEAST ELEVATION

SOUTHWEST ELEVATION

Elevations

087

Well water can form part
of a system to achieve the
independence of a home
from main supply networks
(electricity, gas, and water).

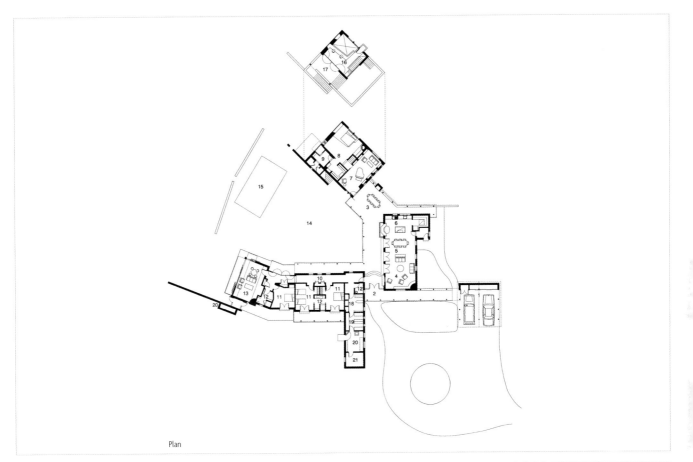

Plan

Balhannah House

The roof of this house faces north to reduce energy consumption during winter. Photovoltaic panels convert sunlight into electrical power and also feed the heating system. An underground water tank was installed that collects water from the roof. The double-glazed joinery with adjustable wooden slats keeps the interior temperature stable.

Architect: Max Pritchard
Architect
Location: Balhannah, Australia
Year of construction: 2008
Photography: Sam Noonan

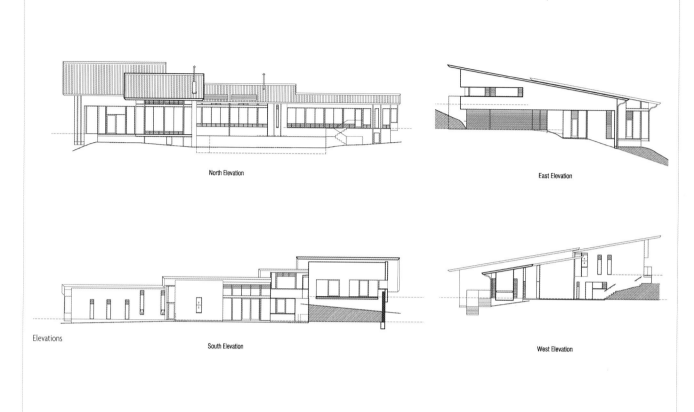

North Elevation

East Elevation

Elevations

South Elevation

West Elevation

The glazed openings in the main facade face north to take advantage of sunlight and distribute energy to the different spaces in the building.

089

Rainwater can be collected on a roof to flow through a spout before it is filtered and stored in a tank. Ideally, water tanks should be underground to prevent algae and bacteria from forming.

090

Airtight joinery will prevent problems in controlled ventilation systems, particularly in large, difficult to cool spaces.

House in Nikaia

This house is divided into two volumes linked by a glass gallery. It is made from recycled, secondhand materials. On the roof, solar panels provide the necessary power, and all lighting is low-consumption LED based. Inside, 33 feet separate the floor from the ceiling—the perfect height to achieve an open space with minimum energy expenditure.

Architect: Christina Zerva Architects
Location: Nikaia, Greece
Year of construction: 2007
Photography: Mihajlo Savic

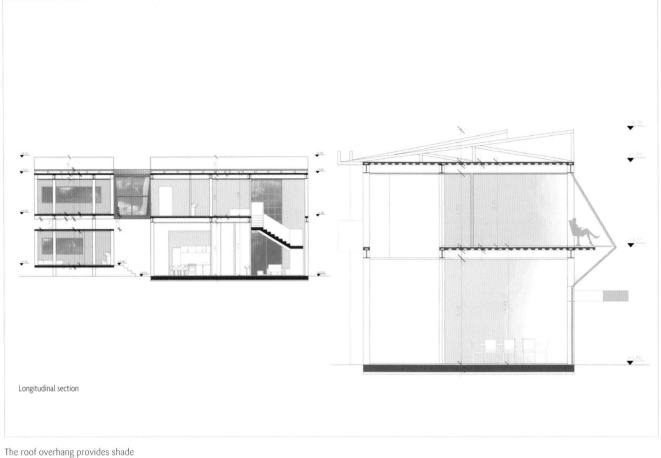

Longitudinal section

The roof overhang provides shade
for the timber deck during hours of
maximum sunshine.

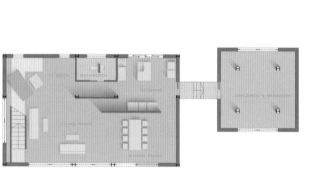

Ground floor plan

091

What is known as the 'greenhouse effect' refers to radiation penetrating glass and heating materials that store heat before releasing it later.

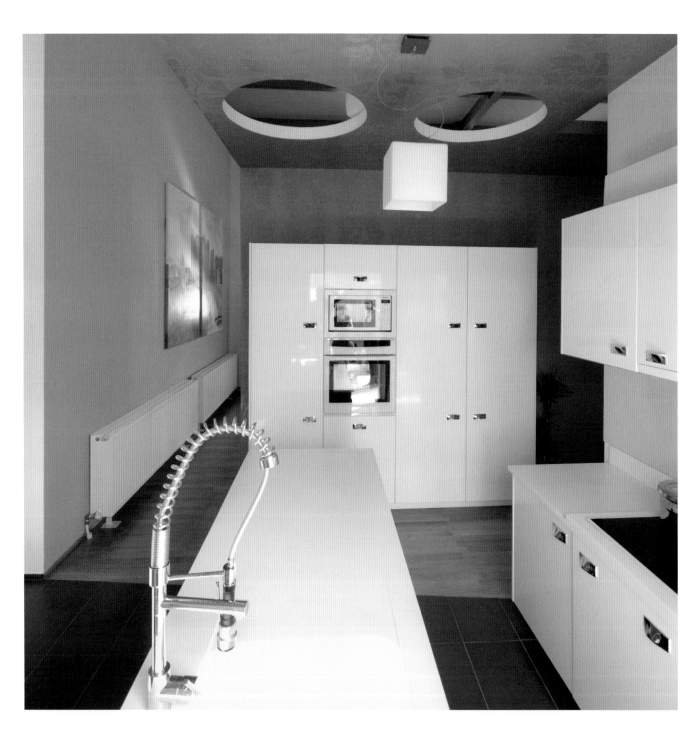

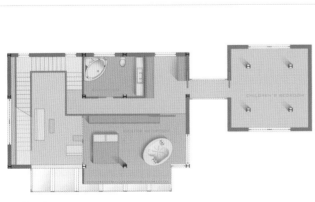

First floor plan

Appliances recommended for the kitchen are: highly insulated refrigerators, energy-efficient dishwashers, glass-ceramic induction stoves, washing machines and tumble dryers with load detection.

Emu Bay House

Architect: Max Pritchard
Architect
Location: Kangaroo Island,
Australia
Year of construction: 2008
Photography: Sam Noonan

This holiday house has two terraces with wooden platforms on both sides of the living room to hold two water systems: a water tank that collects rainwater and an electric heat pump that heats the water. Double-glazed joinery and natural ventilation systems prevent excessive energy consumption.

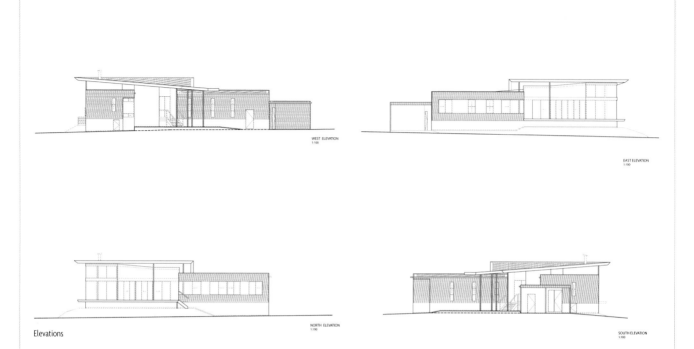

WEST ELEVATION
1:100

EAST ELEVATION
1:100

Elevations

NORTH ELEVATION
1:100

SOUTH ELEVATION
1:100

093

Metal is the most commonly used material for making rainwater storage tanks and cisterns. Galvanized steel is rustproof.

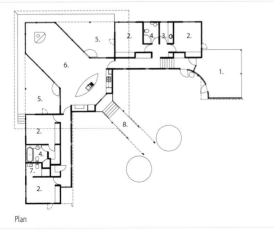

Plan

094

A heat pump uses little power to run, but can be costly to install.

Passive House V.W.

Architect: Franklin Azzi
Architecture
Location: Normandy, France
Year of construction: 2007
Photography: Daniel Moulinet,
Franklin Azzi Architecture

Franklin Azzi Architecture undertook the refurbishment of this former hunting lodge, expanding the space by installing two Cuban army tents. The design includes a system for rainwater collection and for the use of solar and geothermal energy. The body of the structure is made from recycled materials. Wood and vegetable fibers are used to insulate the walls and are placed opposite windows for natural ventilation.

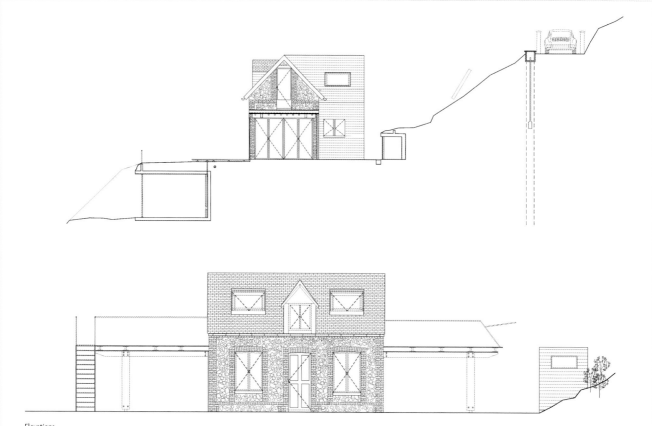

Elevations

095

Good orientation for deck areas can create an energy cushion in winter. A porch can provide protection from the sun in summer.

096

A good air renewal strategy is to have one of the facades always facing the sun and the other in shade to create an air capture inlet on the exterior.

The layout is based on a linear sequence
of spaces associated with the structure,
with large openings and passageways.

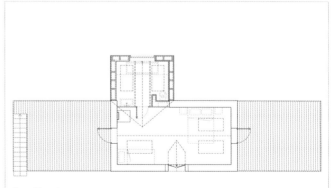

Ground floor plan

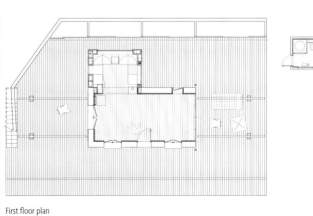

First floor plan

Mona Vale House

Architect: Choi Ropiha
Location: Mona Vale, Australia
Year of construction: 2008
Photography: Simon Whitbred,
Brett Boardman

For this project, the client was interested in developing a sustainable building in collaboration with the Sustainable Energy Development Authority to experiment with a series of active and passive measures. Among the sustainable measures developed were a 15,000 liter rainwater tank, a gray-water recycling system, hydronic radiant floor heating, and photovoltaic solar panels to generate the electricity needed.

East elevation

097

The orientation of energy-capture devices and of the building allows daylight to be filtered.

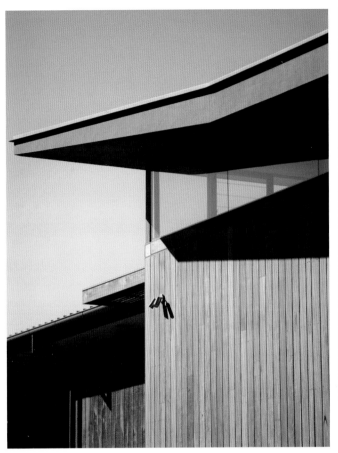

098

The slope of the roof was built in response to the angle of the sun's rays. The choice of clerestory windows in areas with less sunlight allows more light in.

Hydronic radiant heating systems work by means of a boiler that heats and pumps water through a series of pipes laid under the floor.

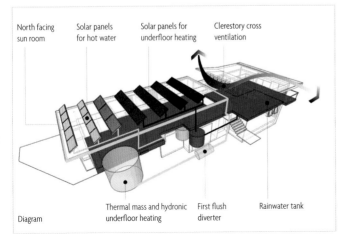

North facing sun room

Solar panels for hot water

Solar panels for underfloor heating

Clerestory cross ventilation

Thermal mass and hydronic underfloor heating

First flush diverter

Rainwater tank

Diagram

Villa Röling

The owners of this house, two art collectors, were looking for a suitable space in which to display their work. The upper level was designed as a wooden box with movable windows to create shade from excessive sunlight on its east, west, and south sides. Water pipes were installed in the concrete floor and connected to a geothermal system, keeping the floor cool in summer and warm in winter.

Architect: Architectenbureau
Paul de Ruiter bv
Location: Kudelstaart,
The Netherlands
Year of construction: 2008
Photography: Pieter Kers

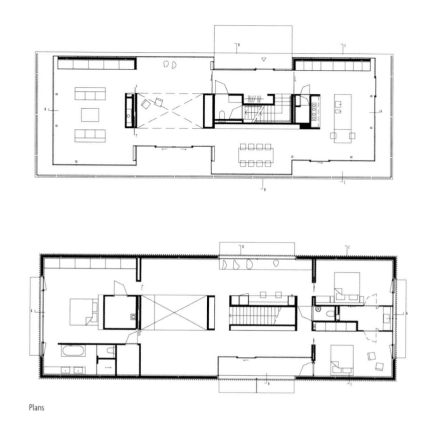

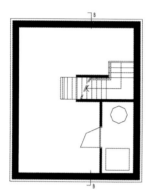

Plans

099

The geothermal system sends heat to or extracts heat from the ground by means of a set of collectors with a water and glycol solution circulating through them that is buried in the subsoil.

100

External sunshades are the most effective way of reducing heat gain through openings and windows.

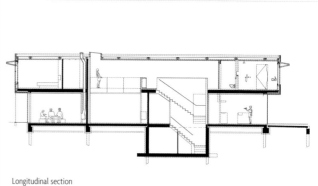

Longitudinal section

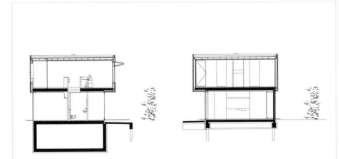

Transversal sections

English Residence

ZeroEnergy Design carried out the remodeling of this home, built in 1958. Challenges involved converting it into a green house, stabilizing temperatures through the underfloor heating, and making the house energy efficient by using renewable energy systems. The floor of the living area is bamboo, the entrance uses travertine, and on the porch and the roof deck, Garapa with FSC organic certified materials are used.

Architect: ZeroEnergy Design
Location: Orleans, MA, USA
Year of construction: 2009
Photography: ZeroEnergy Design

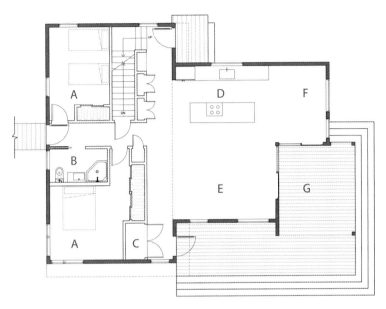

A. Bedroom
B. Bath
C. Laundry
D. Kitchen
E. Living
F. Dining
G. Covered Porch

Ground floor plan

101

Photovoltaic solar panels convert solar radiation into an electric current, which can then be used to power any appliance.

First floor plan

102

The use of natural materials subject to minimum processing will always be more sustainable than synthetic or overly processed materials.

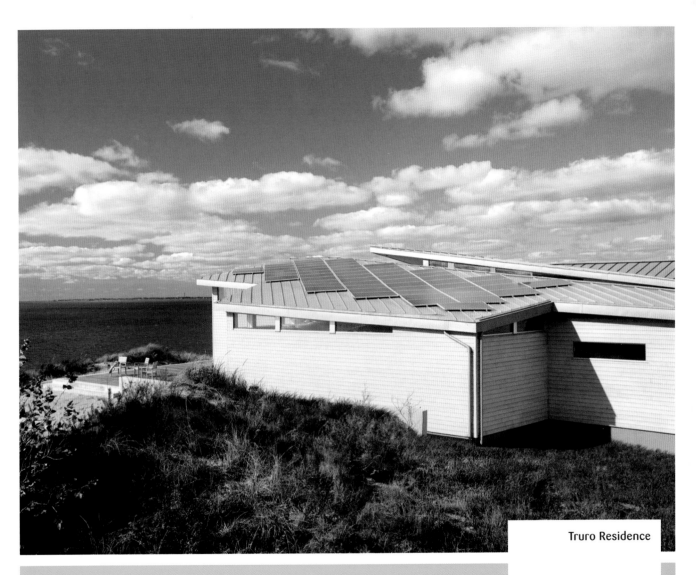

Truro Residence

This house was designed for zero energy consumption. It consumes three times less electricity than a conventional house, because power is generated by solar panels on the south roof. A geothermal system connected to underfloor heating reduces energy consumption for heating. Its materials, such as bamboo, polished concrete, cedar and ipe wood, are durable.

Architect: ZeroEnergy Design
Location: Cape Cod, MA, USA
Year of construction: 2007
Photography: ZeroEnergy Design

103

The best places for glazed expanses are public areas, which can benefit most from sunlight and heat entering.

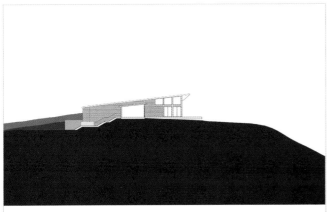

Longitudinal section

104

To make insulation more effective, it is necessary to reduce thermal bridges as much as possible.

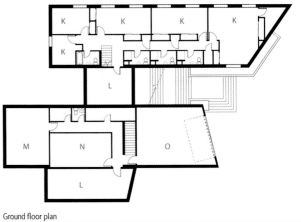

Ground floor plan

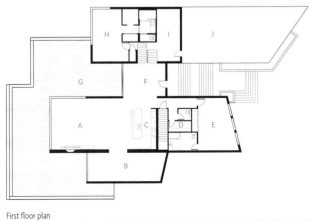

First floor plan

Villa Kram

Villa Kram has been rated the finest Danish green house based on a power calculation program carried out during its design phase. It is home to two families who benefit from living together, but also have their own private spaces. It has solar chimney ventilation that distributes heat throughout the house.

Architect: Manifold, Infusion
Location: Glostrup, Denmark
Year of construction: 2009
Photography: Infusion

Perspective

105

Double glazing improves thermal and acoustic insulation. Window frames that break thermal bridges make the insulation more effective.

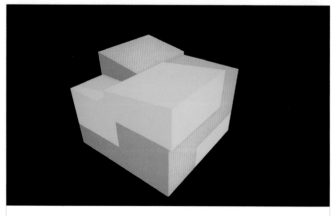

Diagram

106

A well-programmed home automation (domotic) system guarantees an energy efficient system.

Perspective

Prefab Constructions

Pallet House

Pallet House is a low-cost, easy to build house for refugees who have lost their homes for reasons ranging from natural disasters to civil conflicts. Constructed with wooden pallets, the Pallet House is a versatile, economic, sustainable, and recyclable option. A 52 x 52 foot refuge requires one hundred pallets. It adapts to any climate and can be built in less than a week for $3,000.

Architect: I-Beam Design
Year of construction: 2008
Photography: I-Beam Design

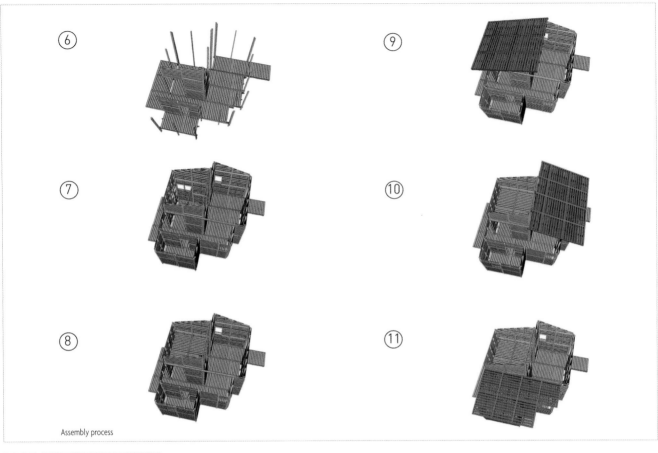

6

7

8

9

10

11

Assembly process

107

Prefabricated homes made of
reused materials allow for easy
disassembly and demolition
if the structure is no longer
needed.

Pallet Houses offers flexibility in their layout, enabling families to build homes that fit their individual needs.

108

Key features of prefabricated
homes are savings in materials,
building time, labor, and costs.

Study Box/Read-Nest

Architect: Dorte Mandrup
Arkitekter ApS
Year of construction: 2008
Photography: Torben Eskerod,
Thomas Mandrup-Poulsen

This small cabin of 105 square feet is intended as an additional space in the garden, to read, sleep, or just to unwind. The exterior is assembled with natural wood slats. The interior has shelves and a fold-out bed, if additional space is needed. Over the bed, the starry sky can be seen through a skylight.

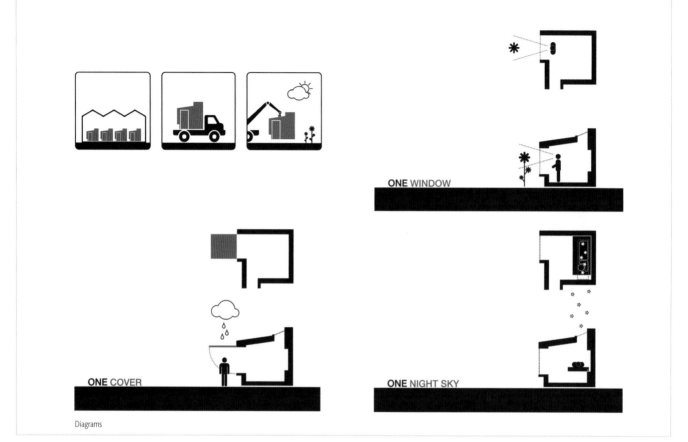

ONE WINDOW

ONE COVER

ONE NIGHT SKY

Diagrams

109

The use of factory-produced prefabricated components assembled on-site is becoming more common.

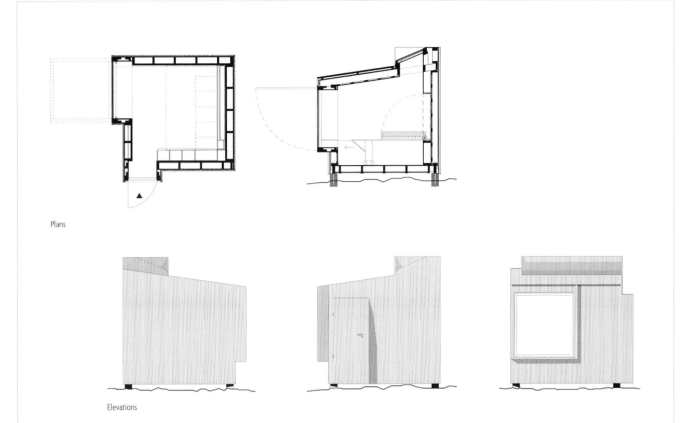

Plans

Elevations

110

Eco-friendly insulation depends on materials used, their thicknesses and positioning.

A skylight and a large window distribute
light evenly throughout the room.

Boxhome

Boxhome is a 205 square foot house with four rooms covering the basic needs of a family: a kitchen/dining room, a bathroom, a living room, and a bedroom. Its skin consists of different layers: wood, glass, wool, a ventilated air chamber, and panels with aluminum finishing. It can be maintained and built with few resources, and it costs a quarter of the price of a similar-sized apartment in Oslo.

Architect: Rintala Eggertsson Architects
Location: Oslo, Norway
Year of construction: 2007
Photography: Ivan Brodey, Pia Ulin, Are Carlsen, Sami Rintala

111

Prefabricated system assembly enables buildings to be designed and built quickly.

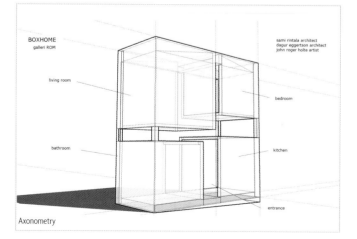

BOXHOME
galleri ROM

sami rintala architect
dagur eggertson architect
john roger holte artist

living room

bedroom

bathroom

kitchen

entrance

Axonometry

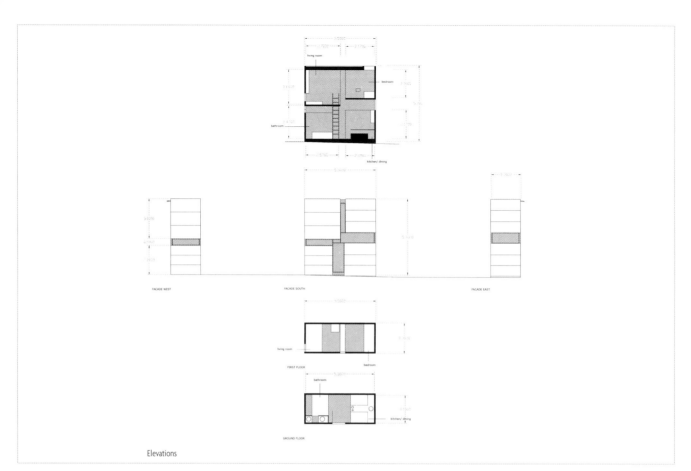

Elevations

112

Interior materials should not give off substance residues or harmful particles that could endanger the health of occupants. Use of synthetic solvents, for instance, needs to be carefully considered.

Morphosis Architects designed The Float House in collaboration with the University of California for Brad Pitt's foundation Make It Right to restore the homes of Hurricane Katrina victims in 2005. The structure is largely prefabricated and uses a substructure of guides that float securely upward to 12.2 feet in the event of flooding.

The Float House

Architect: Morphosis Architects, UCLA Architecture and Urban Design
Location: New Orleans, LA, USA
Year of construction: 2009
Photography: Iwan Baan

Axonometry

ROOF_PHOTOVOLTAIC PANELS
ROOF_STANDING SEAM GALVALUME
ROOF_SIP PANEL
ROOF_SIP OSB
ROOF_SIP FOAM INSULATION
ROOF_SIP FRAMING
ROOF_JOISTS
ROOF_PERFORATED METAL EAVE
ROOF_TIMBERSIL PURLINS
ROOF_STEEL EAVE POSTS

DECK_TIMBERSIL DECKING
DECK_DECORATIVE ALUMINUM
 GUARDRAIL
DECK_PRECAST CONCRETE STAIR

WALL_SWISS PEARL CLADDING
WALL_TIMBERSIL BATTENS
WALL_SIP PANEL

GALLERY_POLYCARBONATE
 CLERESTORY ROOF
RAINWATER COLLECTION TANKS
GALLERY_WINDOW FRAMING
GALLERY_ STEEL DECK SUPPORTS
PHOTOVOLTAIC BATTERY STORAGE
GALLERY_POLYCARBONATE
 HURRICANE SHUTTER

FLOOR PLAN
① FRONT PORCH
② LIVING ROOM
③ GALLERY
④ KITCHEN
⑤ BEDROOM
⑥ BATH
⑦ MECHANICAL
⑧ GUIDE POSTS

113

The roof acts as a filter to guard the interior spaces from aggressive atmospheric agents. Its slope protects against direct sunlight.

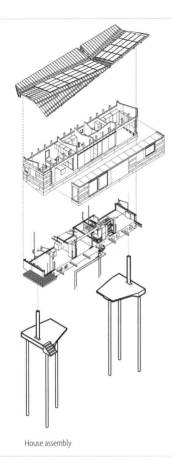

House assembly

Polystyrene was used together with a glass-fiber reinforced concrete. The prototype is designed to be mass-produced and set up anywhere.

114

The balance between natural daylight and control of solar radiation not only improves thermal factors (heat, cold, and moisture), but also electricity use.

Architect: **Studio Makkink & Bey**
Location: **Milan, Italy**
Year of construction: 2009
Photography: **Nicoló Degiorgis,**
Droog

House of Furniture Parts plays with the concepts of content and container. This shed-like structure can be built within a preexisting space, such as an office, loft, or study. It is created using furniture components that are pressed out from the walls and assembled. The components are precut plywood panels, numbered for easy assembly and storage.

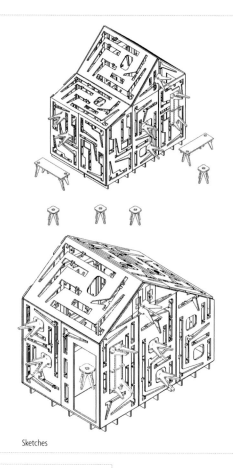

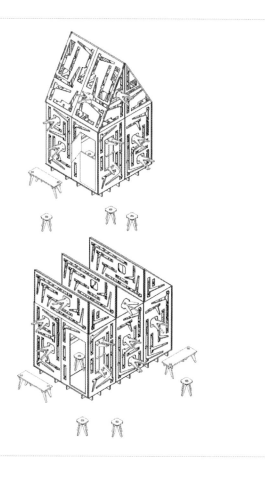

Sketches

115

After a House of Furniture Parts unit is delivered to a building site, a house can be assembled, finished, and occupied in a matter of days.

116

The current prefab trend is to buy a kit that the homeowner can assemble on the desired site.

Flake House is a modular wooden shelter, inspired by the tradition of *follies de bois*, based on prefabricated building solutions. The structure was built entirely in the workshop and is divided into two parts for easy transport by truck. It has two rooms that can be combined in several ways, including the forms of a T-shape or L-shape, or side-by-side.

Architect: Olgga Architectes
Location: Nantes, France
Year of construction: 2009
Photography: Fabienne Delafraye

This project makes effective use of natural resources. It takes into account the effects of the sun, wind, rainfall, and temperature.

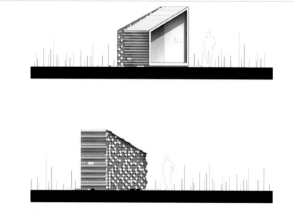

Elevations

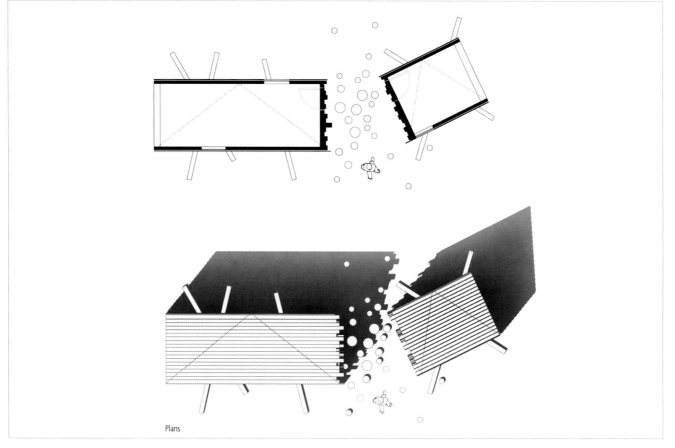

Plans

117

Eco-labeling is a system with labels issued by an official body that guarantees the low environmental impact of material.

Architect: Dorte Mandrup
Architects ApS
Location: Jørlunde, Denmark
Year of construction: 2004
Photography: Torben Eskerod

Raised slightly above ground level, this house includes interior terraces that connect to the outside by moving portable prefabricated perimeter panels. The courtyards are distributed strategically to allow light and heat to penetrate each room of the house.

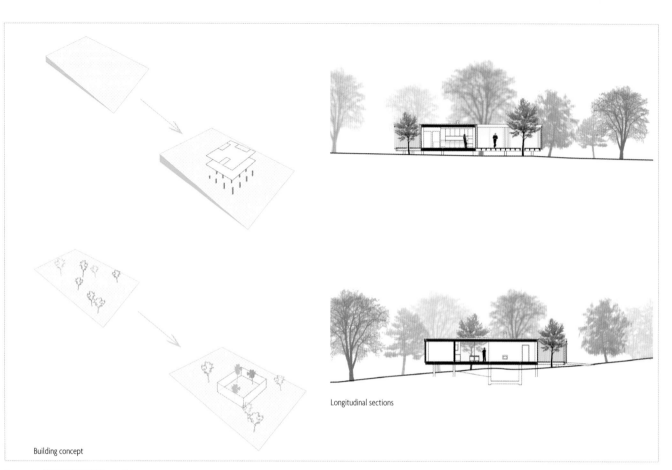

Longitudinal sections

Building concept

118

Accentuating regional and local features, diversity, and adaptability as values in contrast with centralization, will enable natural resources to be enjoyed sustainably.

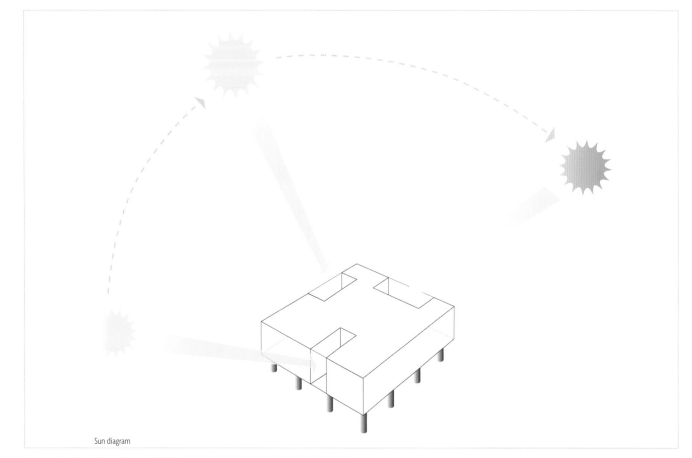

Sun diagram

119

Sliding panels allow new spaces to be obtained that help to cool the atmosphere and light dark corners.

The doors and panels can be kept closed to create a shaded courtyard in summer.

Plan

Sunset Cabin

Architect: Taylor Smyth Architects
Location: Lake Simcoe,
Ontario, Canada
Year of construction: 2004
Photography: Peter
Gumpesberger, Toni
Hafkenscheid

This 323 square foot cabin expands across its terrace toward the lake. Built of cedar and plywood, it took one month to build by furniture makers. It was then dismantled, classified by parts, and reassembled on the lake, which took ten days. The prefabricated building rests on two steel beams supported on four concrete piles so that it does not touch the ground. The roof is vegetated.

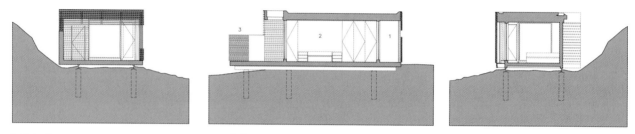

North elevation

Longitudinal section

Transversal section looking north

120

The ease, speed, and water savings provided by dry building systems mean that the entire structure can be assembled in a factory, saving time and reducing building costs.

121

Shutters provide protection from heat and create a second layer of insulation, which is useful in both summer and winter.

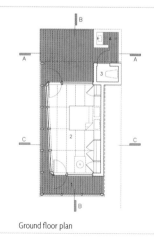

Ground floor plan

The bedroom benefits from the ventilated chamber formed between the wooden slats on the facade and the windows.

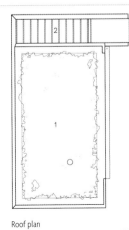

Roof plan

Vermont Cabin

Isolated in an open area of the Green Mountain National Forest in Vermont, this prefabricated home is the refuge for a Brooklyn-based couple. There is no phone and limited cell phone coverage, and it meets all the characteristics of an off-the-grid house. The floors are bamboo and have an underfloor heating system. Electricity is generated by a 3,000 kilowatt solar panel.

Architect: Resolution: 4 Architecture
Location: Jamaica, VT, USA
Year of construction: 2009
Photography: Resolution: 4 Architecture

Electricity is generated by an array of 3,000 kilowatt solar panels located a short distance away from the house.

122

One of the advantages of prefabricated houses is that they can be completely dismantled and transported to another site at their occupants' will.

Plan

123

When prefabricated components arrive on-site, there is little waste produced from packaging or broken pieces.

Garden Studio Mono

Ecospace offers an ecological option for extra space in its gardens. Owners can choose from several ready-made models. They are built with certified cedar wood, have underfloor heating, lighting, and layered insulated SIP panels. The choice to do a green roof is an option.

Architect: **Ecospace**
Location: **mobile**
Year of construction: **2009**
Photography: **Ecospace**

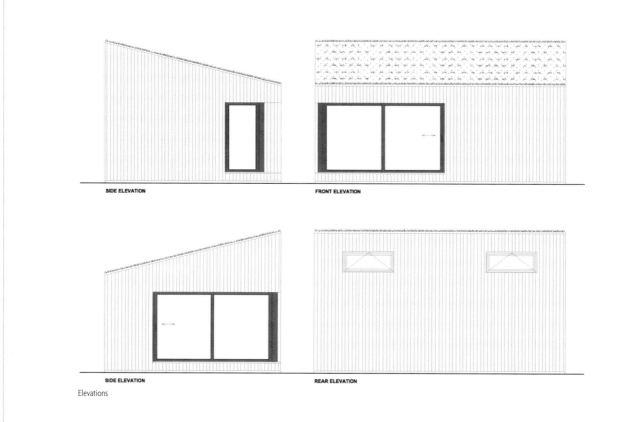

SIDE ELEVATION

FRONT ELEVATION

SIDE ELEVATION

REAR ELEVATION

Elevations

124

Multilayer structural panels on the roofs have a thickness of 9.5 inches.

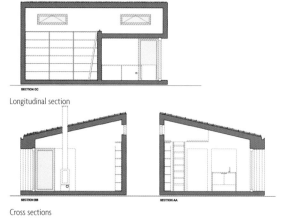

Longitudinal section

Cross sections

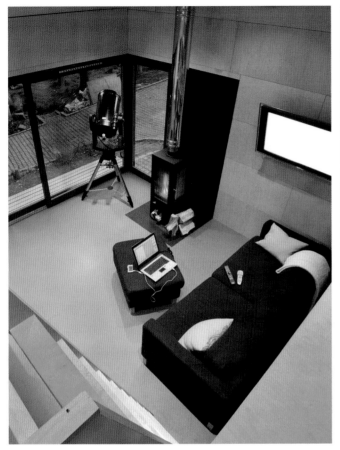

FLOOR PLAN
Plan

MEZZANINE LEVEL

125

Radiant floor heating was the first radiant system linked to hot water produced by solar panels. Radiant wall systems can be used for cooling in summer, with cold water circulation.

Innovative Ideas

JEROEN VAN MECHELEN/© Bjarne Mastenbroek and Jeroen van Mechelen

126

If you are looking for an alternative to heating, you can choose thermal insulation based on a structure made of timber and bubble wrap. This is a low-cost alternative that produces savings on heating.

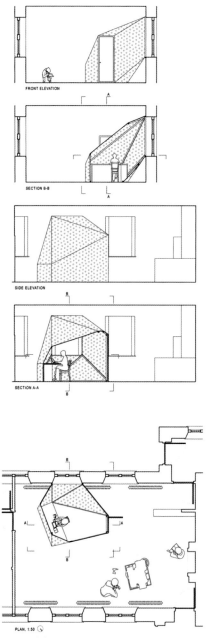

FRONT ELEVATION

SECTION B-B

SIDE ELEVATION

SECTION A-A

PLAN. 1:50

Sections and elevations

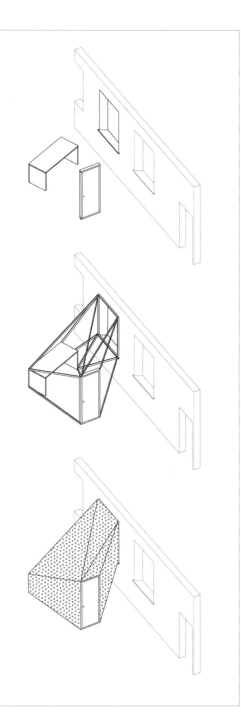

JEROEN VAN MECHELEN/© Bjarne Mastenbroek and Jeroen van Mechelen

127

Instead of covering the entire building with thermal insulation, lower costs by insulating only a particular area of the home with plastic bubble wrap as if it were a cocoon with a timber structure.

JEROEN VAN MECHELEN/© Bjarne Mastenbroek and Jeroen van Mechelen

128

To enter a thermally insulated area, it will be necessary to put in a door. It is recommended to also have a second opening, which may be a window in the same building, in order to ventilate the room.

DAVIDSON RAFAILIDIS/© Steve Mayes Photography

DAVIDSON RAFAILIDIS/© Steve Mayes Photography

129

Cardboard is cheap and easily replacable. Its light weight allows it to easily be used to construct shelves and other structures, and it can be used for mobile architecture.

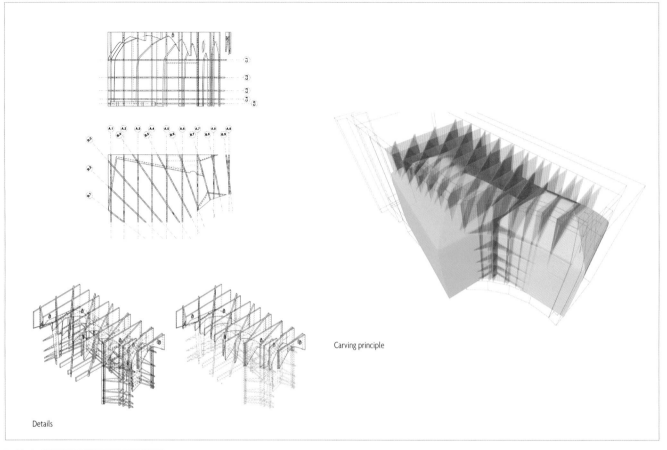

Carving principle

Details

130

In order to make a cardboard cell structure, cardboard with a waterproof wax coating should be used.

DAVIDSON RAFAILIDIS/© Steve Mayes Photography

DAVIDSON RAFAILIDIS/© Steve Mayes Photography

DAVIDSON RAFAILIDIS/© Steve Mayes Photography

131

Cardboard is a material formed by several layers of paper. Its ecological properties with regard to paper include not being bleached (optional) and being recyclable.

132

It is possible to find furnishings made from recycled timber offcuts. The ones featured here were collected from factories in Denmark.

AMY HUNTING/© Amy Hunting

RYAN FRANK / © Ryan Frank

133

Using recycled material repurposes material that already exists. Strata is a line of furniture designed from the wood salvaged from old office desks.

NENDO/© Masayuki Hayashi

NENDO/© Masayuki Hayashi

134

One alternative to recycling the large quantities of waste paper that is thrown away is reuse. Good use can be made of a large roll of paper in the design of a chair. It is as easy as peeling away the paper layers to form the seat.

NENDO/© Masayuki Hayashi

NENDO/© Masayuki Hayashi

NENDO/© Masayuki Hayashi

NENDO/© Masayuki Hayashi

NENDO/© Masayuki Hayashi

NENDO/© Masayuki Hayashi

During the production process, resin is added to reinforce the paper. This chair is recycled and recyclable, and when the chair is no longer required, the paper can be reused.

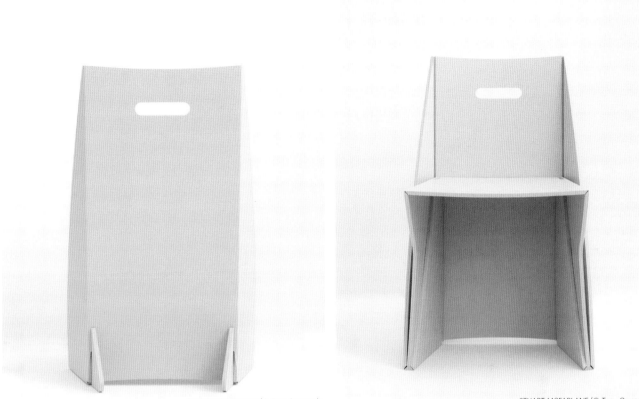

STUART MCFARLANE/© Tony Owczarek

STUART MCFARLANE/© Tony Owczarek

135

A folding chair can be made from 100% recycled plastic. It is easy to assemble and use as no adhesives or screws are necessary.

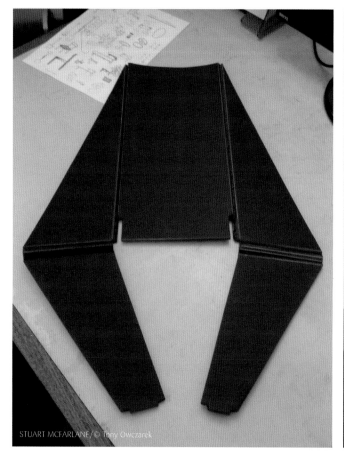

STUART MCFARLANE/© Tony Owczarek

STUART MCFARLANE/© Tony Owczarek

STUART MCFARLANE/© Tony Owczarek

STUART MCFARLANE/© Tony Owczarek

136

You can make your own chair without fasteners or adhesives with a recycled plastic frame that is easy to assemble. Once at the end of its useful life, it can be melted down to make a new chair.

STUART MCFARLANE/© Tony Owczarek

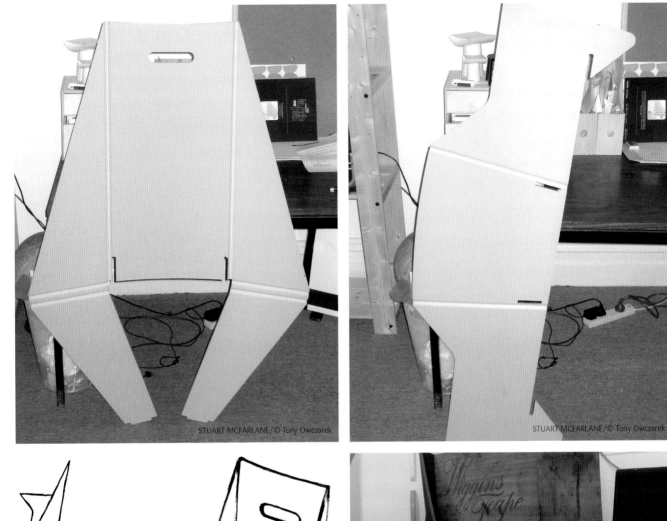

STUART MCFARLANE/© Tony Owczarek

STUART MCFARLANE/© Tony Owczarek

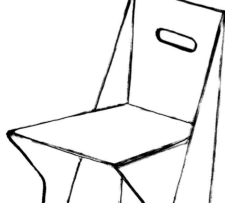

STUART MCFARLANE/© Tony Owczarek

137

Choose furniture made with wood carrying the Forest Stewardship Council (FSC) seal of certification, which guarantees sustainable and controlled exploitation of forestry resources.

JULIA KRANTZ/© Sherry Griffin

JULIA KRANTZ/© Sherry Griffin

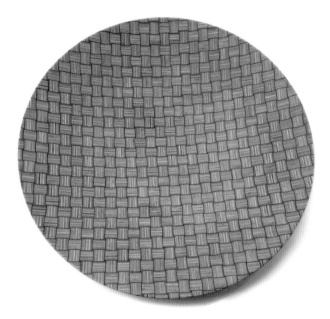

138

Choose decorative details made of wood because it is a renewable raw material that does not harm the environment. It can be recycled without polluting the environment once the end of its life cycle has been reached.

BO REUDLER STUDIO/© Ilco Kemmere and Bo Reudler Studio

BO REUDLER STUDIO/© Ilco Kemmere and Bo Reudler Studio

139

You can reuse forestry log and branch offcuts to handcraft your own furniture.

BO REUDLER STUDIO/© Ilco Kemmere and Bo Reudler Studio

\#1: Idea

\#2 Research

\#3 Collecting

\#4 ... Administration

#5 Sketching

#6 Building

#7 Slow White Series

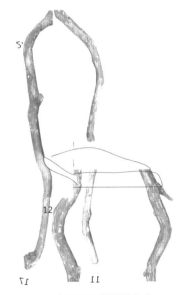

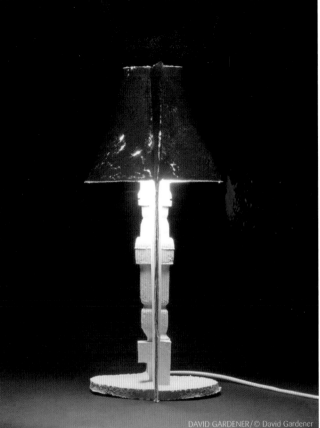

DAVID GARDENER/© David Gardener

DAVID GARDENER/© David Gardener

140

A paste created from recycled newspapers can be used to give life to a lamp featuring a low-energy fluorescent light bulb.

When opened, the packaging becomes
the lampshade, saving on useless waste.

'The Packaging Lamp'®

Warning
For use only with 11W energy saving bulb.

1.

2.

3.

4.

5.

141

Bring new life to an old lamp by making a recycled paper shade with cut-out figures. For better lighting efficiency, use an energy-saving light bulb.

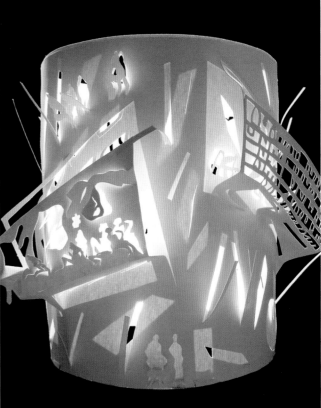

142

There are different lighting alternatives using 100% biodegradable and recycled paper shades. Using easily recyclable materials, such as paper, encourages savings in raw materials and energy.

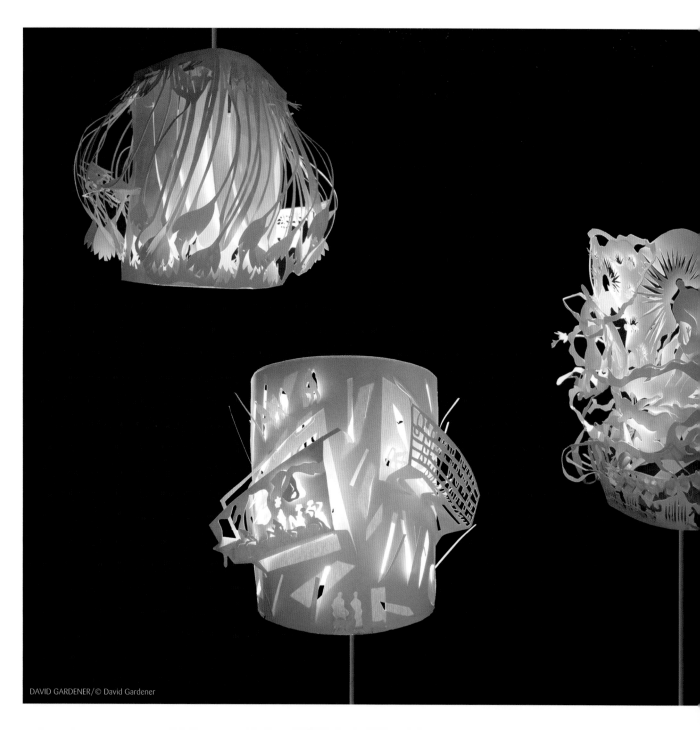

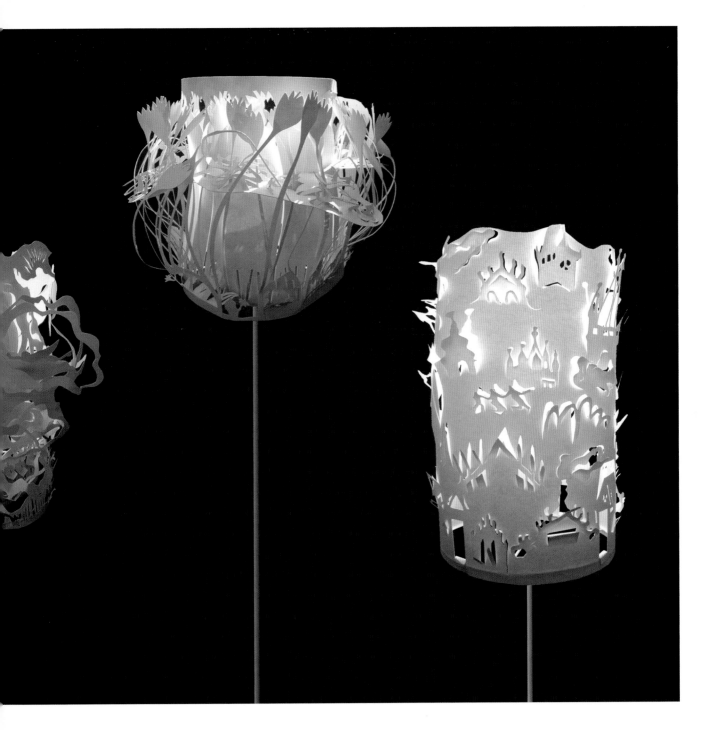

MATHIEU LEHANNEUR and ANTHONY VAN DEN BOSSCHE / © Gaëtan Robillard and Mathieu Lehanneur

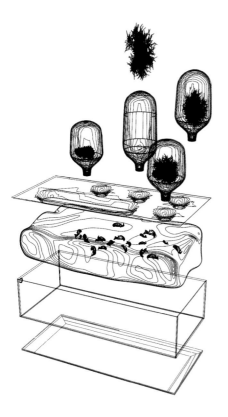

MATHIEU LEHANNEUR and ANTHONY VAN DEN BOSSCHE/
© Gaëtan Robillard and Mathieu Lehanneur

143

A natural ecosystem is possible
in any home. This one is halfway
between an aquarium and a self-
sufficient greenhouse.

MATHIEU LEHANNEUR and ANTHONY VAN DEN BOSSCHE/© Gaetan Robillard and Mathieu Lehanneur

MATHIEU LEHANNEUR and ANTHONY VAN DEN BOSSCHE/© Gaetan Robillard and Mathieu Lehanneur

MATHIEU LEHANNEUR and ANTHONY VAN DEN BOSSCHE / © Gaëtan Robillard and Mathieu Lehanneur

144

Making space for seedlings in an urban garden is easy with products like Hatch, which is made from eggshells.

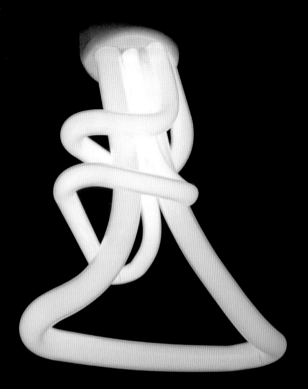
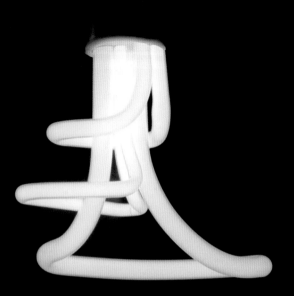
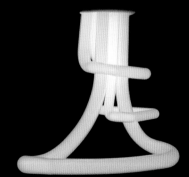
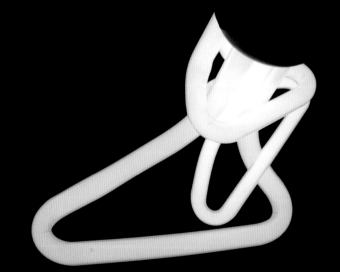

HULGER / © Hannah Jeffery

HULGER/© Hannah Jeffery

HULGER/© Hannah Jeffery

Replacing incandescent light bulbs with energy-saving compact fluorescent bulbs not only gives you noticeable savings at year's end, but, more importantly, reduces greenhouse gas emissions.

146

Low-energy bulbs reduce electricity costs by 80 percent. They last six times longer than conventional incandescent bulbs and make up for their additional cost in less than one year.

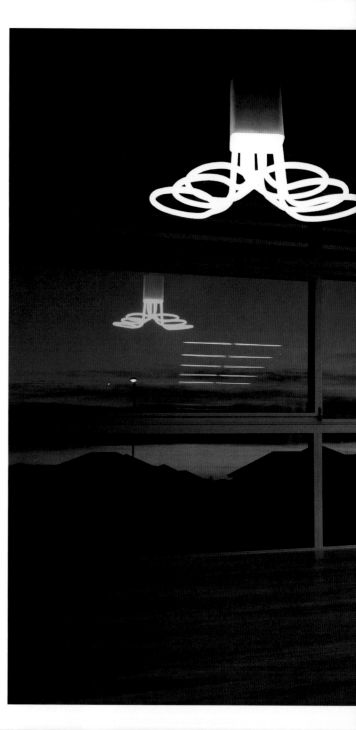

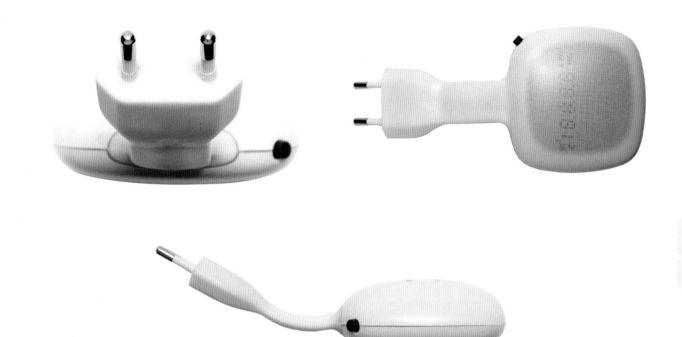

147

One way of controlling energy spending in the home is to install a real-time energy meter, which tells you how much energy you are using at any given time.

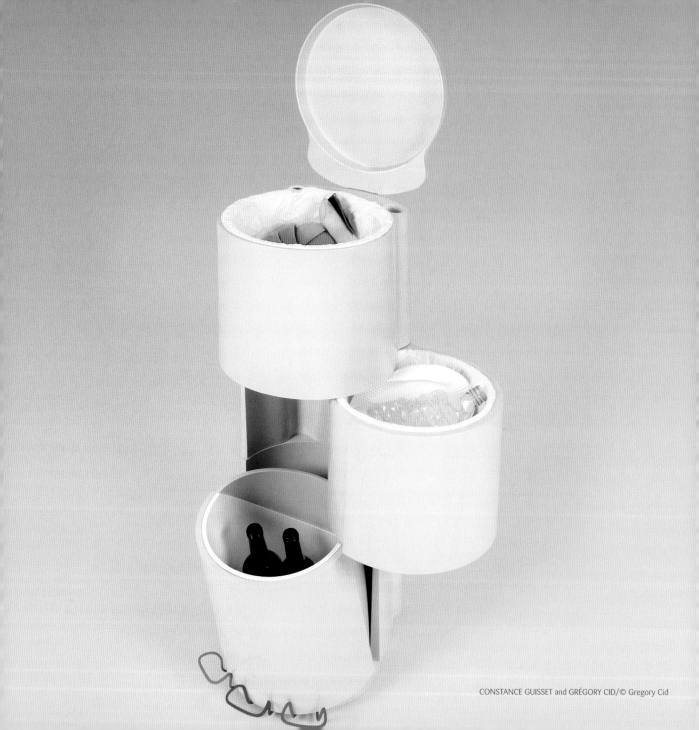

CONSTANCE GUISSET and GRÉGORY CID/© Gregory Cid

CONSTANCE GUISSET and GRÉGORY CID/© Gregory Cid

CONSTANCE GUISSET and GRÉGORY CID/© Gregory Cid

148

It is essential to have articles in the home that make recycling waste easier. This design features three compartments for selective waste disposal.

CONSTANCE GUISSET and GRÉGORY CID/© Gregory Cid

CONSTANCE GUISSET and GRÉGORY CID/© Gregory Cid

CONSTANCE GUISSET and GRÉGORY CID/© Gregory Cid

149

The "rule of the three Rs" encourages reduction, reuse, and recycling of products we consume.

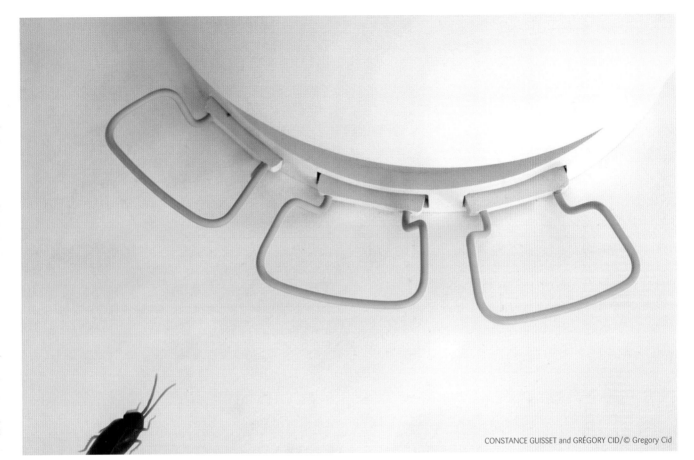

CONSTANCE GUISSET and GRÉGORY CID/© Gregory Cid

CONSTANCE GUISSET and GRÉGORY CID/© Gregory Cid

150

Be aware of the importance of selective waste recycling by avoiding disposable products and packaging, such as cans, sprays and plastics as much as possible as they usually are not biodegradable.